Vegetable Farming Business Plan Template

By Meir Liraz

Publisher: BizMove.com
www.bizmove.com

Copyright © Liraz Publishing. All rights reserved.
ISBN: 9798611067567

Table of Contents

A	Complete Fill In The Blanks Vegetable Farming Business Plan Template	4
B	How to Develop a Results Driven Business Plan	44
C	How to Attract Investors	55
D	How to Obtain Business Loans the Easy Way	64
E	How to Effectively Manage Your Loans	75
F	**Special Free Bonuses (with download instructions):**	84

1. A Word Doc version of the Business Plan Template

2. An Extensive Generic Business Plan Template In MS Word Format

3. A Set of 23 Excel Spreadsheets and Tables

4. Business Feasibility Study System

5. Business Financial Planner (Software Program)

6. How to Improve Your Leadership and Management Skills (eBook)

7. Small Business Management: Essential Ingredients for Success (eBook)

8. How to Create a Business Plan, Training Course (Interactive Video)

9. How To Find And Attract Investors, Training Course (Interactive Video)

10. PowerPoint template to help create a presentation for your business plan

A. Complete Fill in the Blanks Business Plan Template

It is recommended that you download the MS Word Doc version of this template to easily edit and modify it to meet your own specific needs (compatible with most word processors).

The download link is presented at the end of the book; see the first item in the "Special Free Bonuses" section.

Table of Contents
1.0 Executive Summary   1
Chart: Highlights   1
1.1 Objectives   2
1.2 Mission   2
1.3 Keys to Success   2
2.0 Company Summary   2
2.1 Company Ownership   2
2.2 Company History   3
Table: Past Performance   3
Chart: Past Performance   4
3.0 Products   4
4.0 Market Analysis Summary   4
4.1 Market Segmentation   5
Table: Market Analysis   6
Chart: Market Analysis (Pie)   6
4.2 Target Market Segment Strategy   7
4.3 Industry Analysis   7
4.3.1 Competition and Buying Patterns   7
5.0 Strategy and Implementation Summary   7
5.1 SWOT Analysis   7
5.1.1 Strengths   8
5.1.2 Weaknesses   8
5.1.3 Opportunities   8
5.1.4 Threats   8
5.2 Competitive Edge   8
5.3 Marketing Strategy   9
5.4 Sales Strategy   9
5.4.1 Sales Forecast   9

Table: Sales Forecast	10
Chart: Sales Monthly	11
Chart: Sales by Year	11
5.5 Milestones	12
Table: Milestones	12
6.0 Management Summary	12
6.1 Personnel Plan	13
Table: Personnel	13
7.0 Financial Plan	13
7.1 Important Assumptions	14
7.2 Break-even Analysis	14
Table: Break-even Analysis	14
Chart: Break-even Analysis	14
7.3 Projected Profit and Loss	15
Table: Profit and Loss	15
Table: Profit and Loss (Continued)	16
Chart: Profit Monthly	16
Chart: Profit Yearly	16
Chart: Gross Margin Yearly	17
7.4 Projected Cash Flow	18
Table: Cash Flow	18
Chart: Cash	19
7.5 Projected Balance Sheet	19
Table: Balance Sheet	19
Table: Balance Sheet (Continued)	20
7.6 Business Ratios	20
Table: Ratios	21
Table: Sales Forecast	1
Table: Sales Forecast (Continued)	2
Table: Personnel	2
Table: Profit and Loss	3
Table: Cash Flow	4
Table: Balance Sheet	6

1.0 Executive Summary

Company: [Company Name]
Name: [Name]
Address: [Address]
Phone: XXX-XXX-XXXX
Fax: XXX-XXX-XXXX
Email: [Email Address]

[Company Name] is led by owner [Name], who has considerable experience in running an effective business. [Name] has a strong farming background due to his family's farming tradition that dates back to the early 1900's. In 2007 [Name] Farms became [Company Name] after forming a general partnership. The Company is headquartered in Dexter, Missouri where it serves as a row crop business specializing in popcorn, cotton, rice, wheat, soybeans and purple hull peas.

The focus of this business plan is to put forth objectives to make our business stronger, implement new technologies to focus more in detail on financial exponents, to justify payroll for experience and become a role model family farming operation. [Company Name] is ready to elevate to the next step. The Company is seeking grant funding in the amount of $560,000. The funding will be used to purchase trucks and trailers, purchase GPS equipment and purchase new tractors.

Based on the detailed financial projections, [Company Name] future sales for 2010, 2011 and 2012 are expected to be $2,203,949, $2,270,068 and $2,338,170, respectively.

Chart: Highlights

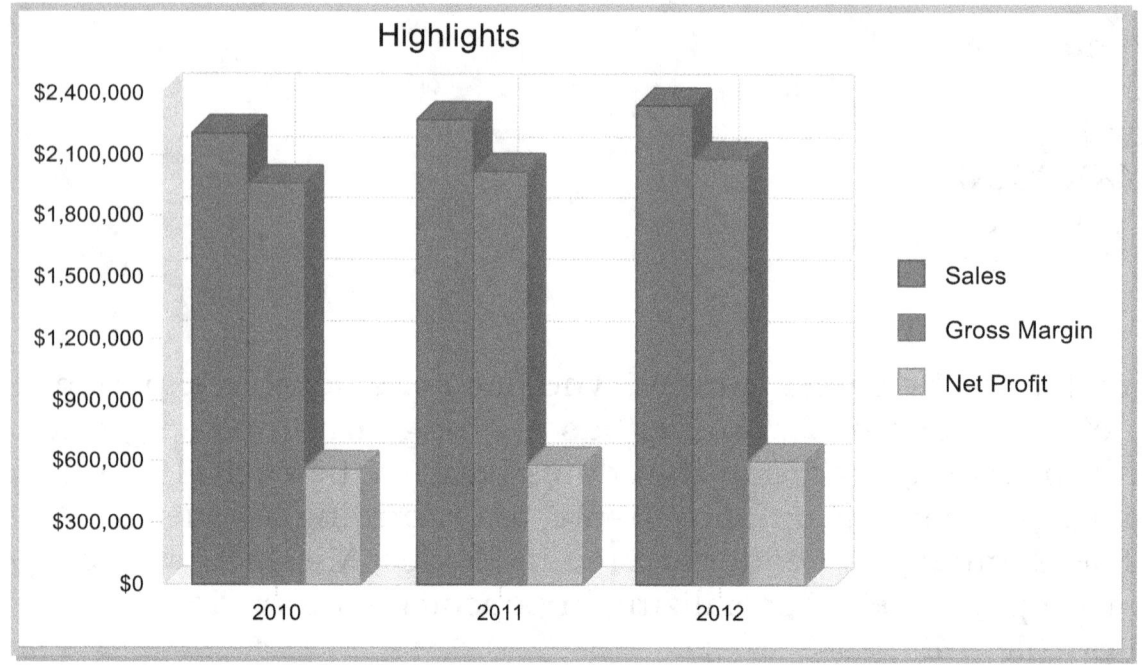

1.1 Objectives

[Company Name] has four main objectives:

- To make our business stronger
- To implement new technologies to focus more in detail on financial exponents
- To justify payroll for experience
- To become a role model family farming operation

1.2 Mission

[Company Name]' mission is to become a strong and self-sustaining farming operation with an interest in educating and offering training and guidance to newer operations; therefore, allowing the Company to give back to the community.

1.3 Keys to Success

[Company Name]' keys to success are:

- To have the ability to grow and strengthen the business to allow proper marketability

- To supply the farming operation with sufficient equipment to allow efficient farming, planting, maintaining and harvesting.

2.0 Company Summary

[Company Name] is headquartered in Dexter, Missouri.

Company: [Company Name]
Name: [Name]
Address: [Address]
Phone: XXX-XXX-XXXX
Fax: XXX-XXX-XXXX
Email: [Email Address]

[Name] Farms was established in 1996 by its owner [Name]. [Name] has a strong farming background due to his family's farming tradition that dates back to the early 1900's. In 2007 [Name] Farms became [Company Name] after forming a general partnership. [Company Name] is a row crop business specializing in popcorn, cotton, rice, wheat, soybeans and purple hull peas. The farm headquarters is located in Dexter, Missouri, which is 25 miles west of the Mississippi River; therefore providing a fertile and well drained farmland.

[Company Name] main crop is cotton, which is very suitable for the area. The farm uses popcorn as a rotation crop because research shows that cotton/corn rotation produces the best yields. Additionally, the farm uses rice on the poorly drained soil and soybeans for that rotation to help on weed control. The wheat and peas are used as a double crop to maximize profit on the un-irrigated land.

2.1 Company Ownership

In 2007 [Name] Farms and [Company Name] formed a general partnership to increase profitability. The owner [Name] controls all interests of the partnership.

2.2 Company History

[Company Name]' sales for 2007, 2008, and 2009 were $856,335, $1,651,482 and $1,472,218, respectively. Earnings for this period were ($104,118), $470,898 and ($23,015), respectively.

2007 was the first year of the partnership, which allowed the Company to double its farmable acres. [Company Name] raised popcorn on all of the new acreage and had an unbelievable yield; therefore, the income in 2008 was the 2007 profit. However, the Company experienced some loss during 2008-2009 due to extreme winds damaging the popcorn crops.

Table: Past Performance

Past Performance			
	2007	2008	**2009**
Sales	$856,335	$1,651,482	**$1,472,218**
Gross Margin	$85,634	$165,148	**$147,222**
Gross Margin %	10.00%	10.00%	**10.00%**
Operating Expenses	$1,095,069	$1,184,187	**$1,633,406**
Collection Period (days)	0	0	**0**
Balance Sheet			
	2007	2008	**2009**
Current Assets			
Cash	($153,345)	($136,670)	**($139,875)**
Accounts Receivable	$12,668	$40,522	**$75,121**
Other Current Assets	$685	$685	**$685**
Total Current Assets	($139,992)	($95,463)	**($64,069)**

Long-term Assets			
Long-term Assets	$1,400	$1,400	**$1,400**
Accumulated Depreciation	$0	$0	**$0**
Total Long-term Assets	$1,400	$1,400	**$1,400**
Total Assets	($138,592)	($94,063)	**($62,669)**
Current Liabilities			
Accounts Payable	$0	$0	**$0**
Current Borrowing	$0	$0	**$0**
Other Current Liabilities (interest free)	$34,474	$460,842	**$406,433**
Total Current Liabilities	$34,474	$460,842	**$406,433**
Long-term Liabilities	$0	$0	**$0**
Total Liabilities	$34,474	$460,842	**$406,433**
Paid-in Capital	$300	$300	**$300**
Retained Earnings	($69,248)	($1,026,103)	**($446,387)**
Earnings	($104,118)	$470,898	**($23,015)**

Total Capital	($173,066)	($554,905)	**($469,102)**
Total Capital and Liabilities	($138,592)	($94,063)	**($62,669)**
Other Inputs			
Payment Days	60	60	**60**
Sales on Credit	$0	$0	**$0**
Receivables Turnover	0.00	0.00	**0.00**

Chart: Past Performance

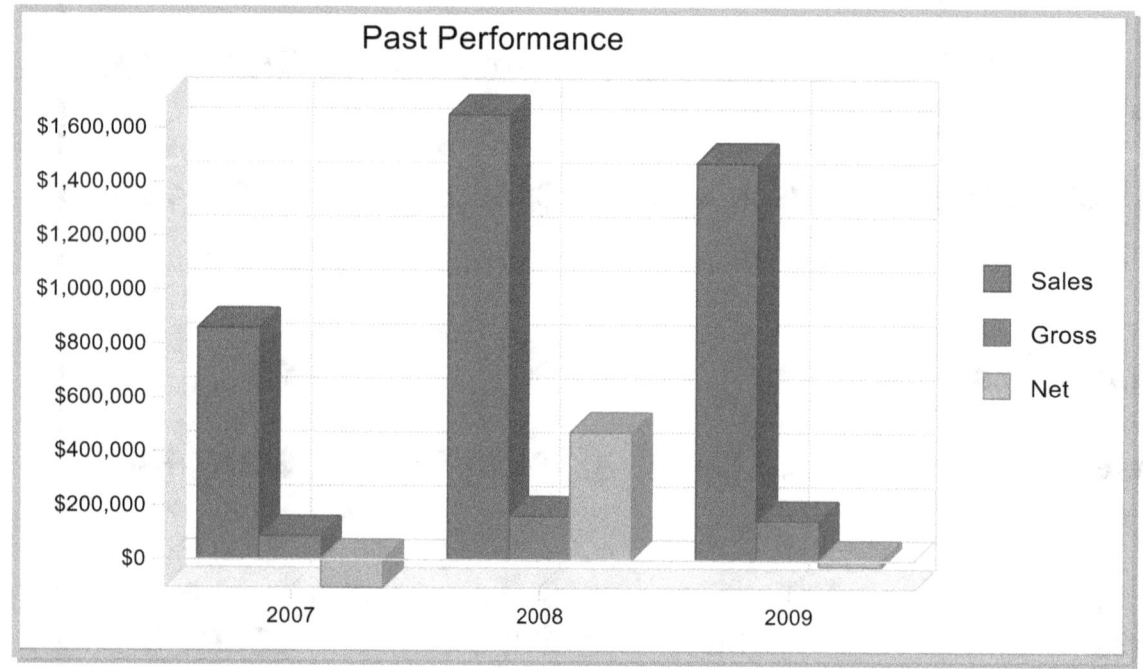

3.0 Products

[Company Name] is a Dexter, Missouri farming service specializing in grain and fiber production. [Company Name] is a high quality row crop business that produces popcorn, cotton, rice, wheat, soybeans and purple hull pea's crops. [Company Name] offers superior products that are suitable for sale and exportation.

4.0 Market Analysis Summary

The US agricultural crop production industry includes more than 1 million farms with combined annual revenue of $175 billion. Crop farming is the growing and harvesting of field crops such as grain, oilseeds, tobacco, dry beans, potatoes, vegetables and melons, fruits and nuts, and floriculture.

Major products within this industry are corn for grain, soybeans, fruits and nuts as well as hay. Other major crops include wheat, vegetables and melons, and cotton and potatoes. Of all farms, 15 percent are grain or oilseed. Grain and oilseed farmers mostly practice crop rotation, typically alternating between plantings of grain corn and soybeans. Planting these crops in succession improves weed control, lowers pest and disease risk and requires less fertilizer.

The overall market for grains and high fiber foods is immense. World whole grain and high fiber foods market is projected to reach about US $21 billion by 2010. This industry has experienced strong growth, aided by healthy demand from livestock industries and an increase in the use of grains in ethanol production. The primary activities of companies in this industry are wheat farming and wheat seed production. Similar Industries include corn farming and grain farming.

[Company Name] business plan focuses solely on the grain and fiber market. [Company Name] has all the needed potential to flourish within this market. The Company has been a highly productive farm showing high yields each season.

4.1 Market Segmentation

[Company Name] is located in Dexter, Stoddard County, Missouri. The local market consists of the Dexter and Stoddard County population, while the expanded market consists of the national US population. Both populations are reached through the local elevators we sell to.

The following information was obtained from Wikipedia.

City Of Dexter-Demographics

As of the census of 2000, there were 7,356 people, 3,237 households, and 2,019 families residing in the city. The population density was 1,208.0 people per square mile (466.4/km²). There were 3,560 housing units at an average density of 584.6/sq mi (225.7/km²). The racial makeup of the city was 97.31% White, 0.15% African American, 0.46% Native American, 0.18% Asian, 0.50% from other races, and 1.40% from two or more races. Hispanic or Latino of any race were 1.20% of the population.

There were 3,237 households out of which 29.4% had children under the age of 18 living with them, 47.0% were married couples living together, 12.1% had a female householder with no husband present, and 37.6% were non-families. 33.8% of all households were made up of individuals and 17.7% had someone living alone who was 65 years of age or older. The average household size was 2.23 and the average family size was 2.83.

In the city the population was spread out with 23.7% under the age of 18, 9.2% from 18 to 24, 25.9% from 25 to 44, 20.9% from 45 to 64, and 20.3% who were 65 years of age or older. The median age was 39 years. For every 100 females there were 82.2 males. For every 100 females age 18 and over, there were 77.3 males.

The median income for a household in the city was $23,116, and the median income for a family was $32,175. Males had a median income of $26,724 versus $17,409 for females.

The per capita income for the city was $15,034. About 14.8% of families and 18.3% of the population were below the poverty line, including 23.5% of those under age 18 and 16.3% of those age 65 or over.

County of Stoddard-Demographic

As of the census of 2000, there were 29,705 people, 12,064 households, and 8,480 families residing in the county. The population density was 36 people per square mile (14/km²). There were 13,221 housing units at an average density of 16 per square mile (6/km²). The racial makeup of the county was 97.34% White, 0.91% Black or African American, 0.40% Native American, 0.09% Asian, 0.01% Pacific Islander, 0.24% from other races, and 1.01% from two or more races. 0.78% of the population were Hispanic or Latino of any race. 38.4% were of American, 15.4% German, 12.4% Irish and 8.5% English ancestry according to Census 2000.

There were 12,064 households out of which 30.50% had children under the age of 18 living with them, 57.40% were married couples living together, 9.40% had a female householder with no husband present, and 29.70% were non-families. 26.60% of all households were made up of individuals and 13.70% had someone living alone who was 65 years of age or older. The average household size was 2.39 and the average family size was 2.88.

In the county the population was spread out with 23.90% under the age of 18, 8.50% from 18 to 24, 26.30% from 25 to 44, 24.10% from 45 to 64, and 17.20% who were 65 years of age or older. The median age was 39 years. For every 100 females there were 92.60 males. For every 100 females age 18 and over, there were 88.20 males.

The median income for a household in the county was $33,120, and the median income for a family was $41,072. Males had a median income of $26,514 versus $17,778 for females. The per capita income for the county was $18,003. About 12.80% of families and 16.50% of the population were below the poverty line, including 20.20% of those under age 18 and 17.60% of those age 65 or over.

All of our customers exist due to our professional reputation as well as through the long-standing relationship we've developed. Our customers appreciate our homegrown crops.

These customers have the option to do business with other farmers within the area, but they understand that working with [Company Name] is beneficial to them because we deliver the dedication and outstanding products that they desire.

[Company Name]' local market is reflected in the Market Analysis Table below.

Table: Market Analysis

Market Analysis							
		2010	2011	2012	2013	2014	
Potential Customers	Growth						CAGR
Dexter	0%	7,356	7,356	7,356	7,356	7,356	**0.00%**
Stoddard	0%	29,537	29,537	29,537	29,537	29,537	**0.00%**
Total	**0.00%**	**36,893**	**36,893**	**36,893**	**36,893**	**36,893**	**0.00%**

Chart: Market Analysis (Pie)

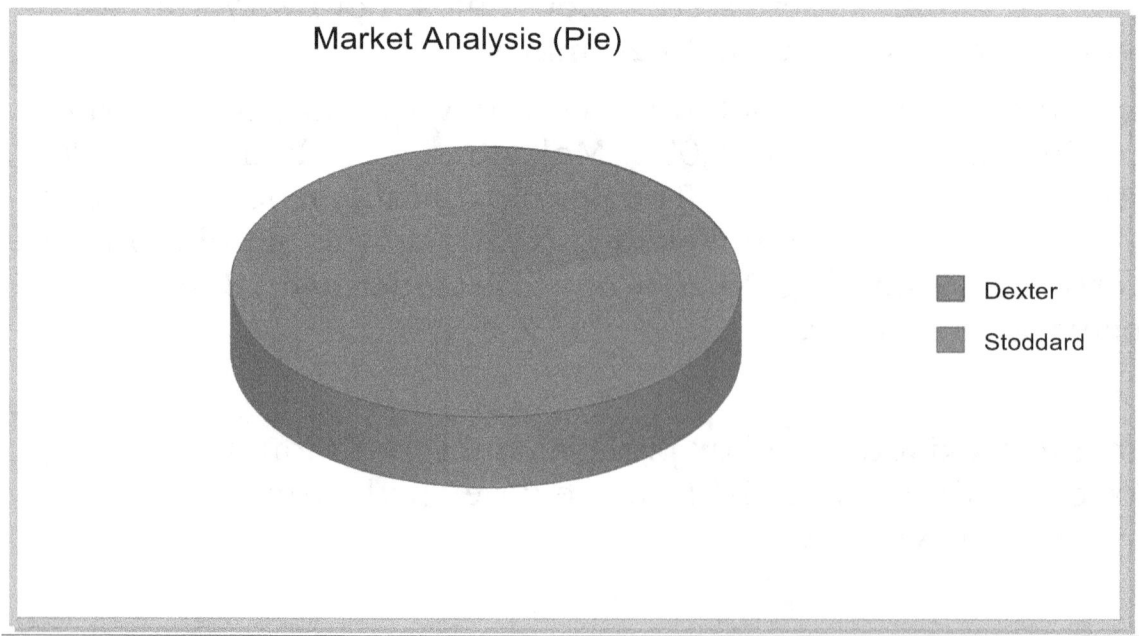

4.2 Target Market Segment Strategy

[Company Name]' mission is to remain a strong and self-sustaining farming operation. The Company has an interest in obtaining more land, equipment and manpower to increase its competitive edge.

Currently, [Company Name]' serves the grain and fiber market segment. [Company Name]' choice of target markets is based on comprehensive experience within the crop farming industry coupled with an in-depth understanding of the customer's needs. [Company Name]' skills and capabilities have allowed the Company to effectively compete and establish a reputation within its area. However obtaining grant funding will improve the Company's productivity and profitability levels.

4.3 Industry Analysis

The agriculture industry plays a vital role in the U.S economy. It supplies the country with a wide variety of food products and non-food products and it remains one of the Nation's larger industries in terms of total employment. [Company Name] knows that its target customers are concerned with quality of product; thus the Company has built its reputation on providing customers with exceptional yield. Our commodity is available for the customer when they need it.

   4.3.1 Competition and Buying Patterns

[Company Name] exist in a purely competitive market. The competition is endless and larger farms reap more benefits. Although, the Company's has experienced hardship due to its size and past crop failure, the Company's longevity and industry experience has enabled it to succeed in the grain and fiber industry. With proper funding, the Company can become stronger and have more eating equity by obtaining more land and equipment to maximize production.

5.0 Strategy and Implementation Summary

[Company Name] have clearly defined the target market and have differentiated itself by offering a solid solution to fulfilling its customers' needs. Reasonable sales targets have been established with an implementation plan designed to ensure the goals set forth below are achieved.

5.1 SWOT Analysis

The SWOT analysis aids in displaying the internal strengths and weaknesses that [Company Name] must address. It allows us to examine the opportunities presented to [Company Name] as well as potential threats. The company's **strength** will help it to succeed. These strengths are: having an outstanding reputation, strong farming background and industry knowledge, excellent and stable staff that helps the business runs efficiently, perseverance and longevity. Strengths are valuable, but it is also important to realize the **weaknesses** [Company Name] must address. [Company Name]' main weakness is limited cash flow and resources, the inability to embrace technology and have dependable equipment, and lacking the means to transport to the market.

5.1.1 Strengths

[Company Name] has much notable strength. These strengths include:

- Outstanding Reputation
- Strong farming background and industry experience
- Excellent and stable staff that helps the business runs efficiently
- Perseverance and longevity

5.1.2 Weaknesses

[Company Name] has a few weaknesses. These weaknesses include:

- Limited cash flow and resources
- The inability to embrace technology and have dependable equipment
- Lacking the means to transport to the market

5.1.3 Opportunities

Opportunities for [Company Name] include using new and more productive, efficient farming practices, and raising new commodities. Ongoing education is an important opportunity for [Company Name] to stay up to date with the latest farming practices that would make our business more productive and efficient.

The opportunity for raising new commodities may introduce itself in the future, due to market demands.

5.1.4 Threats

Weather is our main threat, which can either work for us or against us. Too much moisture, not enough moisture, and hail storms are some examples of weather threats. National and global economic troubles do not threaten the need for our products, but do threaten profit potential. Weeds, insects and disease are also potential threats to the crop that we work on controlling throughout the farming season. Additional threats include competition from established farming businesses and outside investors with cash.

5.2 Competitive Edge

[Company Name]' competitive edge is our in-depth knowledge, seasoned staff and our longevity in the farming industry. By building a business based on long-standing relationships with satisfied clients, we simultaneously build defenses against competition. The longer the relationship stands, the more we help our clients understand what we offer them and why they need it. Furthermore, [Company Name] focuses on making the business sustainable by making practical, educated decisions.

5.3 Marketing Strategy

Currently, [Company Name] has an advantage because the owner, [Name] is a superior business man and a diligent worker that offers years of industry knowledge to the grain and fiber industry. [Name] has a strong farming background; in fact, his family has been in the farming industry since 1901. Furthermore, [Company Name] has made many strong relationships which have allowed the Company to build a reputation in the grain and fiber industry. The farming operation knows what its customers need and the quality that they desire; thus, it aims to satisfy them.

5.4 Sales Strategy

The owner of [Company Name] has excellent work ethics and knows all the ins and outs of the grain and fiber industry. He effectively leads his team to maximize productivity and to ensure good yield results. These are the skills which have been useful in aiding the Company to achieve high sales goals. Additionally, keeping customers happy, we feel, is an implicit part of building a relationship that will encourage repeat business.

The sales forecast monthly summary is included in the appendix. The annual sales projections are included here in Table below.

5.4.1 Sales Forecast

[Company Name]' average monthly sales for rice are $2083 during the months of March-November. The Company's annual total sales for rice are forecast to be $18,750.

[Company Name]' average monthly sales for cotton are $144,711 during the months of March-November. The Company's annual total sales for cotton are forecast to be $1,302,399.

[Company Name]' average monthly sales for purple hull peas are $25,000 during the months of March-November. The Company's annual total sales for purple hull peas are forecast to be $225,000.

[Company Name]' average monthly sales for popcorn are $54,000 during the months of March-November. The Company's annual total sales for popcorn are forecast to be $486,000.

[Company Name]' average monthly sales for wheat are $13,889 during the months of March-November. The Company's annual total sales for wheat are forecast to be $125,000.

[Company Name]' average monthly sales for soybeans are $5,200 during the months of March-November. The Company's annual total sales for cotton are forecast to be $46,800.

The 2010 forecast for [Company Name]' total sales are $2,203,949. During the years 2011 and 2012 the Company will see a 3% annual increase.

Table: Sales Forecast

Sales Forecast			
	2010	2011	**2012**
Unit Sales			
Rice	3,750	3,863	**3,978**
Cotton	2,034,999	2,096,049	**2,158,930**
Purple Hull Peas	12,500	12,875	**13,261**
Popcorn	3,240,000	3,337,200	**3,437,316**
Wheat	25,000	25,750	**26,523**
Soybeans	5,200	5,356	**5,517**
Total Unit Sales	5,321,449	5,481,092	**5,645,525**
Unit Prices	2010	2011	**2012**
Rice	$5.00	$5.00	**$5.00**
Cotton	$0.64	$0.64	**$0.64**
Purple Hull Peas	$18.00	$18.00	**$18.00**
Popcorn	$0.15	$0.15	**$0.15**
Wheat	$5.00	$5.00	**$5.00**
Soybeans	$9.00	$9.00	**$9.00**

Sales			
Rice	$18,750	$19,313	**$19,892**
Cotton	$1,302,399	$1,341,471	**$1,381,715**
Purple Hull Peas	$225,000	$231,750	**$238,703**
Popcorn	$486,000	$500,580	**$515,597**
Wheat	$125,000	$128,750	**$132,613**
Soybeans	$46,800	$48,204	**$49,650**
Total Sales	$2,203,949	$2,270,068	**$2,338,170**
Direct Unit Costs	2010	2011	**2012**
Rice	$0.50	$0.50	**$0.50**
Cotton	$0.06	$0.06	**$0.06**
Purple Hull Peas	$1.80	$1.80	**$1.80**
Popcorn	$0.01	$0.02	**$0.02**
Wheat	$0.50	$0.50	**$0.50**
Soybeans	$0.90	$0.90	**$0.90**
Direct Cost of Sales			
Rice	$1,875	$1,931	**$1,989**
Cotton	$130,240	$134,147	**$138,172**

Purple Hull Peas	$22,500	$23,175	**$23,870**
Popcorn	$48,600	$50,058	**$51,560**
Wheat	$12,500	$12,875	**$13,261**
Soybeans	$4,680	$4,820	**$4,965**
Subtotal Direct Cost of Sales	**$220,395**	**$227,007**	**$233,817**

Chart: Sales Monthly

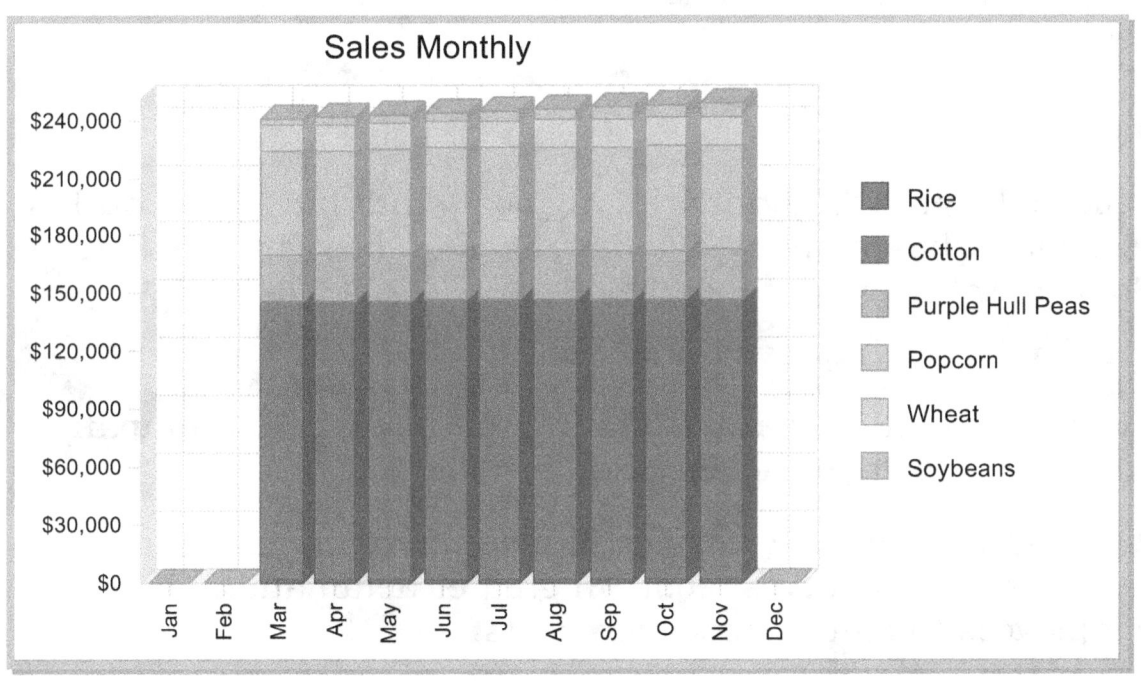

Chart: Sales by Year

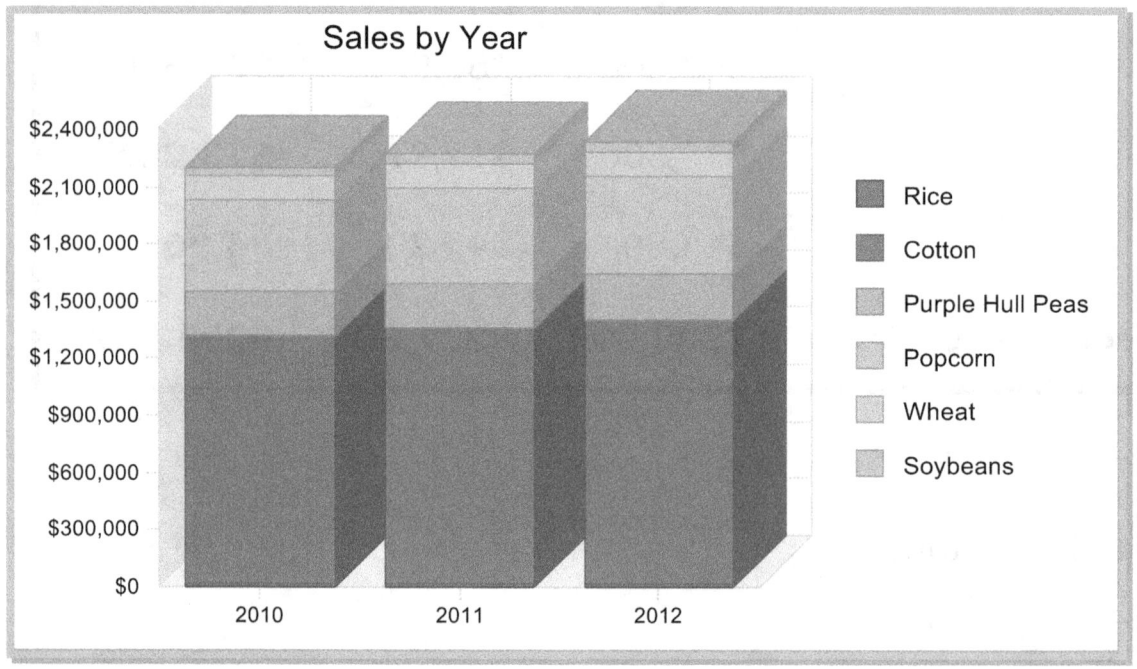

5.5 Milestones

In order to achieve the growth and marketing goals that have been outline in this business plan, the Company has deadlines to meet and ideas to implement. Some of these are outlined below:

- Obtain grant funding to improve business.

- Purchase new trucks and trailers. Updating these will help [Company Name] become more energy efficient and limit breakdowns.

- Purchase GPS equipment. Use of this will help us to streamline and accurately input plant to harvest costs in greater detail and reduce fatigue of employees to reduce operation costs.

- Get new tractors. In order to utilize GPS technology, we have to update our machinery. The new tractors will also give employees incentive because the equipment will be more reliable.

Table: Milestones

Milestones				
Milestone	Start Date	End Date	Budget	**Manager**
Purchase new truck and trailers	7/5/2010	11/1/2010	$70,000	[Name]
Purchase GPS equipment	7/5/2010	11/1/2010	$80,000	[Name]
Get tractors	7/5/2010	11/1/2010	$350,000	[Name]
Totals			**$500,000**	

6.0 Management Summary

[Company Name] is owned and operated by [Name]. The company, being small in nature, requires a simple organizational structure. Implementation of this organizational form calls for the owner, Mr. Hampton, to make the major management decisions in addition to monitoring other business activities.

[Company Name]' office manager is Brian Crawford. Mr. Crawford has a Masters in Business Administration. The supervisor is Andy Keating, who has 40 years of experience within the industry. The additional workforce includes three laborers; [Name] , [Name] and [Name] .

The team's weakness in key management functions exist due to labor issues. If the laborers lack experience, they have to be trained thoroughly, which soaks up plenty of valuable time.

[Company Name] organizational structure

[Name]----->Brian Crawford---->Andy Keating----.>Laborers

6.1 Personnel Plan

The table below contains the details of our personnel plan. The detailed monthly personnel plan for the first year is included in the appendix.

[Name] is the owner and manager of [Company Name]. The Company is a seasonal business that only operates during the months of March-November.

[Company Name] has six employees. The Company consists of the owner, the office manager, the supervisor and three laborers.

The office manager receives an annual salary of $11,232. The supervisor receives an annual salary of 15,444. Two experienced laborers receive an annual salary of 14,040, while the new laborer has an annual salary of $11,934. The salary will increase in 2011 and 2012 by 3%

A future goal of the Company would be to hire a shop foreman to help with repairs and keep the Company productive.

Table: Personnel

Personnel Plan			
	2010	2011	**2012**
Office Manager	$11,232	$11,569	**$11,916**
Supervisor	$15,444	$15,907	**$16,385**
[Name] -Laborer	$14,040	$14,461	**$14,895**
[Name] -Laborer	$11,934	$12,292	**$12,661**
[Name] -Laborer	$14,040	$14,461	**$14,895**
Total People	5	5	**5**
Total Payroll	**$66,690**	**$68,691**	**$70,751**

7.0 Financial Plan

The current financial plan for [Company Name] is to obtain grant funding in the amount of $560,000. The grant will be used to purchase trucks and trailers, GPS equipment and new tractors. The additional cash will go towards the Company's working capital.

The following sections of this plan will serve to describe [Company Name] financial plan in more detail:

- General Assumptions
- Break-even Analysis
- Profit and Loss
- Cash Flow
- Balance

7.1 Important Assumptions

The table below presents the assumptions used in the financial calculations of this business plan.

[Company Name]' average per-unit revenue is estimated to be $0.41. The average per-unit variable cost is estimated to be $0.04. The estimated monthly fixed cost is $96,311.

7.2 Break-even Analysis

For the Company's break-even analysis, the monthly unit's break-even is projected to be 258,351. The monthly revenue break-even is projected to be $107,012. The break-even analysis has been calculated on the "burn rate" of The Company. [Company Name] feels that this gives the investor a more accurate picture of the actual risk of the venture.

Table: Break-even Analysis

Break-even Analysis	
Monthly Units Break-even	258,381
Monthly Revenue Break-even	$107,012
Assumptions:	
Average Per-Unit Revenue	$0.41
Average Per-Unit Variable Cost	$0.04
Estimated Monthly Fixed Cost	$96,311

Chart: Break-even Analysis

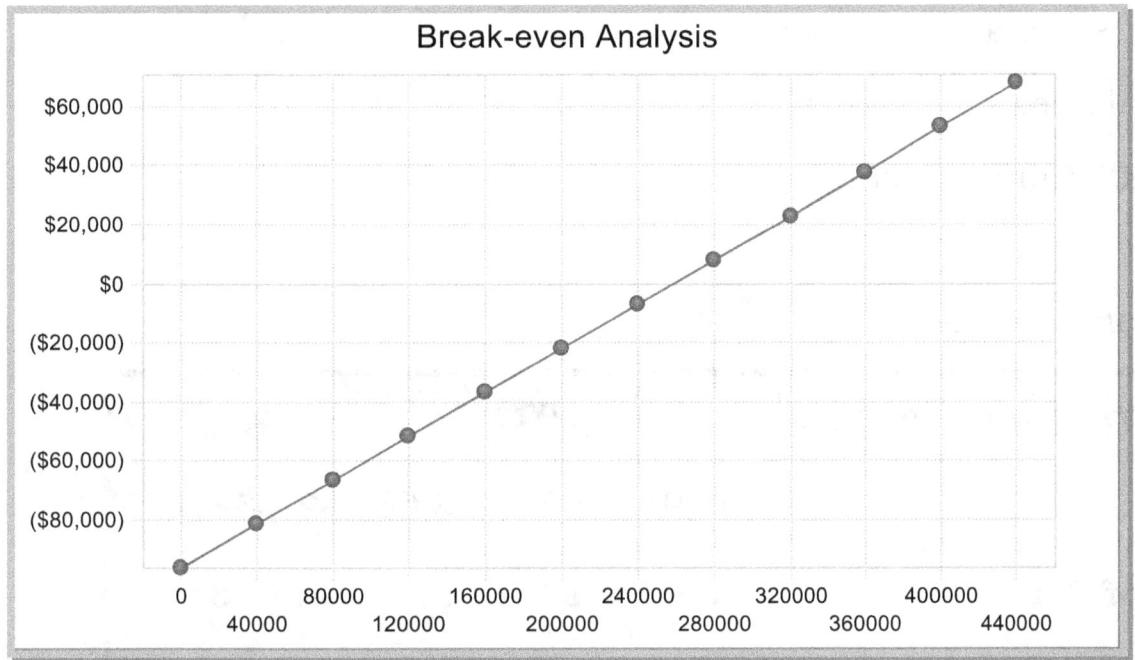

7.3 Projected Profit and Loss

[Company Name]' Pro Forma Profit and Loss statement was constructed from a conservative point-of-view, and is based in large part on past performance.

The sales for 2010, 2011 and 2012 are $2,203,949, $2,270,068 and $2,338,170, respectively. The net profit for the same period is $565,130, $586,057 and $607,641, respectively. The percentages of the net profit sales for this period were 25.64%, 25.82% and 25.99%, respectively.

Once the Company receives grant funding to add the new assets, the depreciation of the new fixed assets will be over a five year period and is depreciated by 20%. Since the truck and trailers, GPS and tractors totaled $560,000, its then divided by five years and equals $100,000 a year. The depreciation for 2011 and 2012 will be calculated using straight-line depreciation.

The aggregated amount of miscellaneous expenses is 30% of the total sales. The miscellaneous expenses consist of:

- Medical Expense
- Interest Expense
- Dues and Membership Fees

- Office Supplies
- Equipment Purchase
- Professional Fees
- Repairs and Maintenance
- Taxes

Table: Profit and Loss

Pro Forma Profit and Loss	2010	2011	2012
Sales	$2,203,949	$2,270,068	**$2,338,170**
Direct Cost of Sales	$220,395	$227,007	**$233,817**
Other Costs of Sales	$22,039	$22,701	**$23,382**
Total Cost of Sales	$242,434	$249,707	**$257,199**
Gross Margin	$1,961,515	$2,020,360	**$2,080,971**
Gross Margin %	89.00%	89.00%	**89.00%**
Expenses			
Payroll	$66,690	$68,691	**$70,751**
Marketing/Promotion	$0	$0	**$0**
Depreciation	$99,996	$100,000	**$100,000**
Rent	$238,536	$245,692	**$253,063**
Utilities	$32,049	$33,010	**$34,001**

Insurance	$47,268	$48,686	**$50,147**
Payroll Taxes	$10,004	$10,304	**$10,613**
Other	**$661,185**	**$681,020**	**$701,451**

Table: Profit and Loss (Continued)

Total Operating Expenses	**$1,155,727**	**$1,187,403**	**$1,220,025**
Profit Before Interest and Taxes	$805,788	$832,957	**$860,946**
EBITDA	$905,784	$932,957	**$960,946**
Interest Expense	($1,541)	($4,268)	**($7,113)**
Taxes Incurred	$242,199	$251,167	**$260,418**
Net Profit	$565,130	$586,057	**$607,641**
Net Profit/Sales	**25.61%**	**25.82%**	**25.99%**

Chart: Profit Monthly

Chart: Profit Yearly

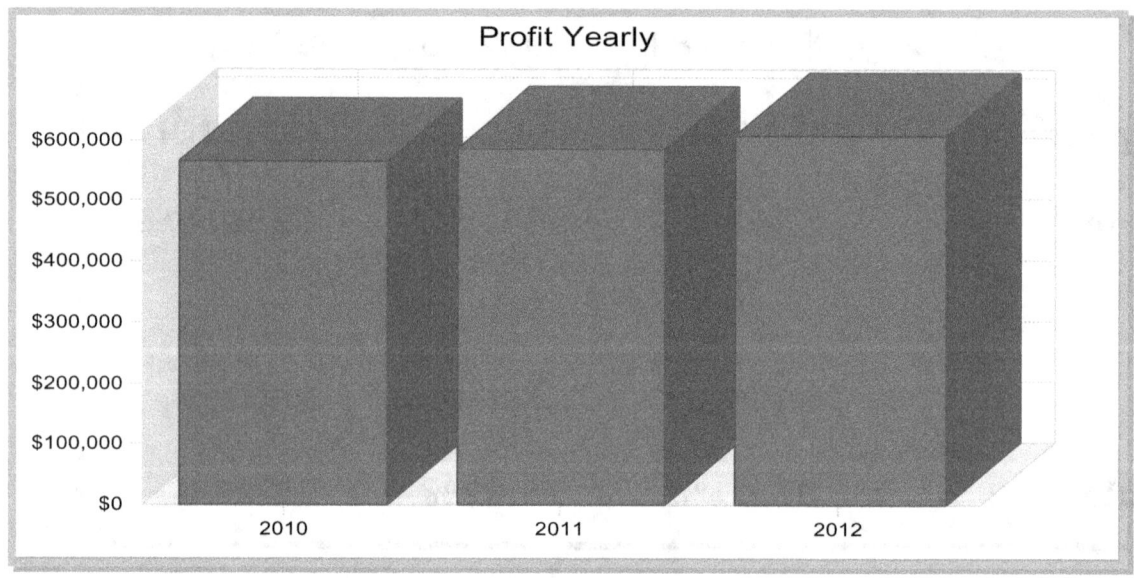

Chart: Gross Margin Monthly

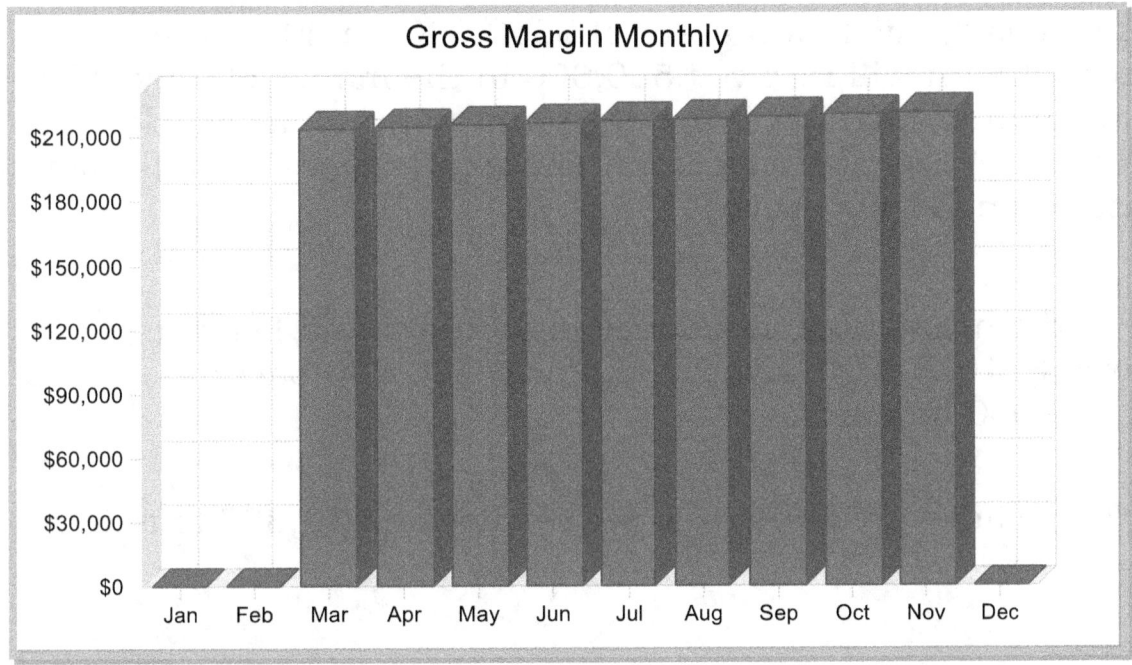

Chart: Gross Margin Yearly

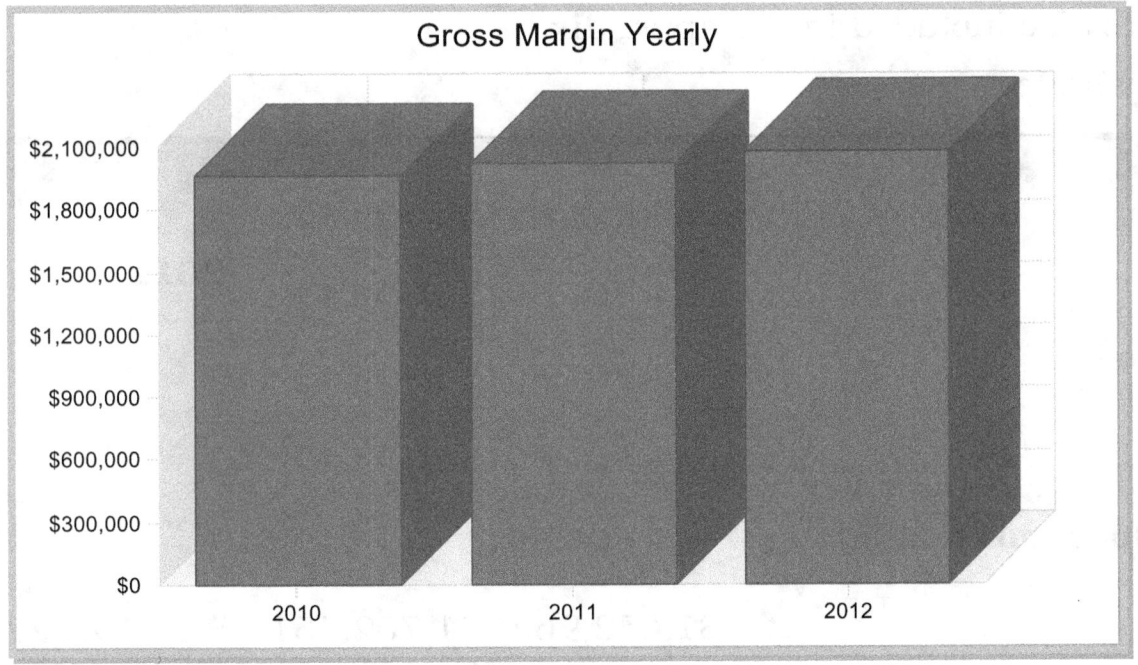

7.4 Projected Cash Flow

[Company Name] has applied for a grant of $560,000. In 2010, the Company forecast that it will receive $560,000 in the month of July. After receipt of the Grant Funding, it will use the grant to purchase trucks and trailers, GPS equipment and new tractors. These purchases are reflected in the purchase of long-term assets.

The Company had a negative cash balance in January and February; thus, it borrowed $110,000 in January and paid $40,000 back in February and $70,000 in March.

The Company's liabilities are $406,433. We've allocated $3,387 to reduce principle.

The following table displays [Company Name]' cash flow and the chart illustrates monthly cash flow in the first year. Monthly cash flow projections are also included in the appendix.

Table: Cash Flow

Pro Forma Cash Flow	2010	2011	2012
Cash Received			
Cash from Operations			
Cash Sales	$1,652,962	$1,702,551	**$1,753,627**
Cash from Receivables	$566,021	$565,714	**$582,686**
Subtotal Cash from Operations	$2,218,983	$2,268,265	**$2,336,313**

Additional Cash Received			
Sales Tax, VAT, HST/GST Received	$0	$0	**$0**
New Current Borrowing	$110,000	$0	**$0**
New Other Liabilities (interest-free)	$0	$0	**$0**
New Long-term Liabilities	$0	$0	**$0**
Sales of Other Current Assets	$0	$0	**$0**
Sales of Long-term Assets	$0	$0	**$0**
New Investment Received	$560,000	$0	**$0**
Subtotal Cash Received	$2,828,983	$2,268,265	**$2,336,313**
Expenditures	2010	2011	**2012**
Expenditures from Operations			
Cash Spending	$66,690	$68,691	**$70,751**
Bill Payments	$1,468,499	$1,395,037	**$1,556,123**
Subtotal Spent on Operations	$1,535,189	$1,463,728	**$1,626,875**
Additional Cash Spent			
Sales Tax, VAT, HST/GST Paid	$0	$0	**$0**

Out			
Principal Repayment of Current Borrowing	$110,000	$0	**$0**
Other Liabilities Principal Repayment	$0	$0	**$0**
Long-term Liabilities Principal Repayment	$40,644	$40,644	**$40,644**
Purchase Other Current Assets	$0	$0	**$0**
Purchase Long-term Assets	$560,000	$0	**$0**
Dividends	$0	$0	**$0**
Subtotal Cash Spent	$2,185,833	$1,504,372	**$1,667,519**
Net Cash Flow	$643,150	$763,893	**$668,794**
Cash Balance	**$563,275**	**$1,267,168**	**$1,935,963**

Chart: Cash

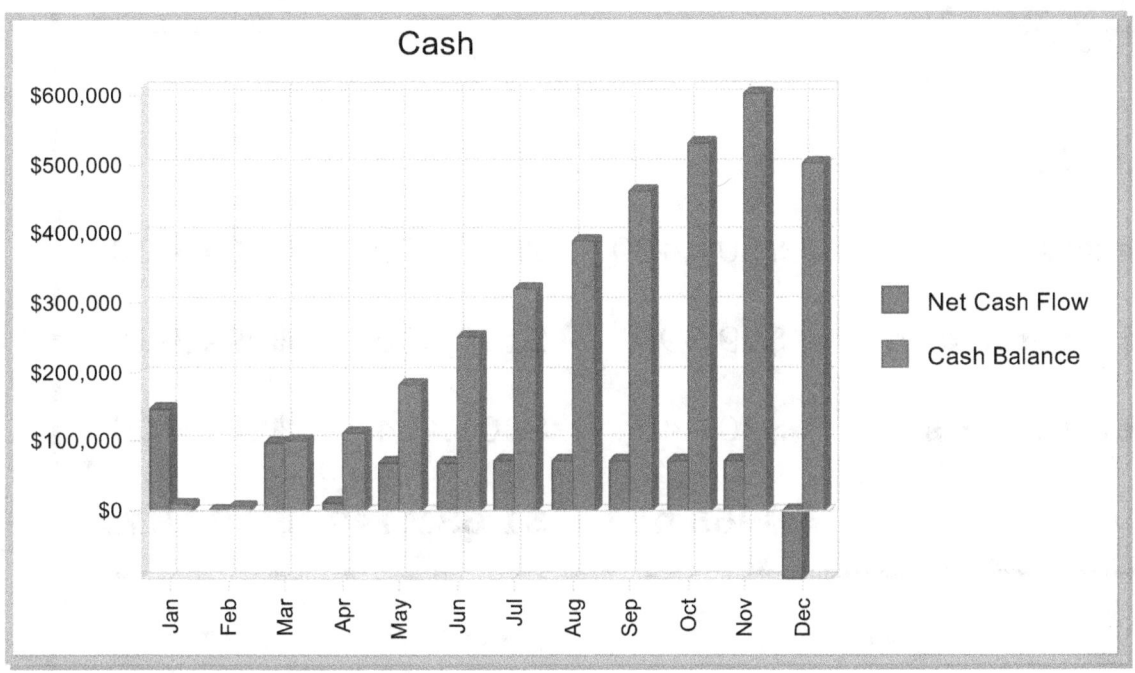

7.5 Projected Balance Sheet

[Company Name] net worth is $$595,398, $1,181,455 and $1,789,096, for 2010, 2011, and 2012, respectively.

Table: Balance Sheet

Pro Forma Balance Sheet			
	2010	2011	**2012**
Assets			
Current Assets			
Cash	$503,275	$1,267,168	**$1,935,963**
Accounts Receivable	$60,087	$61,890	**$63,747**
Other Current Assets	$685	$685	**$685**

Total Current Assets	$564,047	$1,329,743	**$2,000,394**
Long-term Assets			
Long-term Assets	$501,400	$501,400	**$501,400**
Accumulated Depreciation	$99,996	$199,996	**$299,996**
Total Long-term Assets	$401,404	$301,404	**$201,404**
Total Assets	**$965,451**	**$1,631,147**	**$2,201,798**

Table: Balance Sheet (Continued)

Liabilities and Capital	2010	2011	2012
Current Liabilities			
Accounts Payable	$4,264	$124,547	**$128,201**
Current Borrowing	$0	$0	**$0**
Other Current Liabilities	$406,433	$406,433	**$406,433**
Subtotal Current Liabilities	$410,697	$530,980	**$534,634**
Long-term Liabilities	($40,644)	($81,288)	**($121,932)**
Total Liabilities	$370,053	$449,692	**$412,702**
Paid-in Capital	$500,300	$500,300	**$500,300**
Retained Earnings	($469,402)	$95,098	**$681,155**
Earnings	$564,500	$586,057	**$607,641**
Total Capital	$595,398	$1,181,455	**$1,789,096**
Total Liabilities and Capital	$965,451	$1,631,147	**$2,201,798**
Net Worth	**$595,398**	**$1,181,455**	**$1,789,096**

7.6 Business Ratios

The table below presents the projected business ratios from the grain farming markets as a reference.

Table: Ratios

Ratio Analysis	2010	2011	2012	Industry Profile
Sales Growth	49.70%	3.00%	3.00%	**11.78%**
Percent of Total Assets				
Accounts Receivable	6.22%	3.79%	2.89%	**4.53%**
Other Current Assets	0.07%	0.04%	0.03%	**30.39%**
Total Current Assets	58.48%	81.53%	90.86%	**42.98%**
Long-term Assets	41.52%	18.47%	9.14%	**57.02%**
Total Assets	100.00%	100.00%	100.00%	**100.00%**
Current Liabilities	-41.54%	-17.27%	-12.63%	**17.05%**
Long-term Liabilities	-4.20%	-4.98%	-5.54%	**44.58%**
Total Liabilities	-45.74%	-22.26%	-18.17%	**61.63%**
Net Worth	145.74%	122.26%	118.17%	**38.37%**
Percent of Sales				

Sales	100.00%	100.00%	100.00%	**100.00%**
Gross Margin	89.00%	89.00%	89.00%	**69.14%**
Selling, General & Administrative Expenses	63.36%	63.18%	63.01%	**12.86%**
Advertising Expenses	0.00%	0.00%	0.00%	**0.33%**
Profit Before Interest and Taxes	36.56%	36.69%	36.82%	**4.25%**
Main Ratios				
Current	-1.41	-4.72	-7.19	**1.47**
Quick	-1.41	-4.72	-7.19	**0.99**
Total Debt to Total Assets	-45.74%	-22.26%	-18.17%	**61.63%**
Pre-tax Return on Net Worth	57.30%	41.97%	33.35%	**9.43%**
Pre-tax Return on Assets	83.51%	51.31%	39.41%	**3.62%**

Additional Ratios	2010	2011	2012	
Net Profit Margin	25.64%	25.82%	25.99%	n.a
Return on Equity	40.11%	29.38%	23.35%	n.a
Activity Ratios				
Accounts Receivable Turnover	9.17	9.17	9.17	n.a
Collection Days	62	39	39	n.a
Accounts Payable Turnover	302.08	12.17	12.17	n.a
Payment Days	28	16	30	n.a
Total Asset Turnover	2.28	1.39	1.06	n.a
Debt Ratios				
Debt to Net Worth	-0.31	-0.18	-0.15	n.a
Current Liab. to Liab.	0.00	0.00	0.00	n.a
Liquidity Ratios				
Net Working Capital	$966,846	$1,612,259	$2,279,256	n.a
Interest Coverage	0.00	0.00	0.00	n.a

Additional Ratios				
Assets to Sales	0.44	0.72	0.94	n.a
Current Debt/Total Assets	-42%	-17%	-13%	n.a
Acid Test	0.00	0.00	0.00	n.a
Sales/Net Worth	1.56	1.14	0.90	n.a
Dividend Payout	**0.00**	**0.00**	**0.00**	n.a

B. How to Develop a Result Driven Business Plan

There are many reasons why a business plan should be prepared. Each is sufficient by itself for why one must go through the exercise of preparing the actual business plan. This guide discusses free small business plans, business plan outline. Regardless of the specific reason, the underlying goal of preparing a business plan is to insure the success of the business. Here are the main reasons why a business plan should be prepared:

Provides you with the road map that you need in order to run your business. It allows you to make detours, change directions, and alter the pace that you set in starting or running the business.

To assist in financing. Whether one is starting up a small business or is an entrepreneur, banks and financial institutions want to see that you know where you are, where you are going, and how you are going to get there.

The plan will tell you how much money you need, when you will need it, and how you are going to get it. In other words, how you will do your financing?

Helps you to clearly think through what type of business you are starting, and allows you to consider every aspect of that business.

Raises the questions that you need to have answered in order to succeed in your business.

Establishes a system of checks and balances for your business so that you avoid mistakes.

Sets up bench marks to keep your business under control.

Helps you develop the competitive spirit to make you keenly prepared and ready to operate.

Makes you think through the entire business process so that you do not open the business blindly or lack vital information in opening and maintaining your business.

Forces you to analyze competition.

Will give you a "go" or "no go" answer about starting the business.

Small Business Plans Business Plan Outline Guide

Below is an outline for a business plan. Use this model as a guide when developing the business plan for your business.

Elements of a Business Plan Outline:

1. Cover sheet
2. Executive Summary
3. Table of contents

A. The Business

(1) Description of business

(2) Marketing

(3) Competition

(4) Operating procedures

(5) Personnel

(6) Financial data

B. Financial Data

(1) Loan applications

(2) Capital equipment and supply list

(3) Balance sheet

(4) Break-even analysis

(5) Pro-Forma income projections (profit & loss statements)

* Three-year summary

* Detail by month first year

* Detail by quarters, second and third years

* Assumptions upon which projections were based

(6) Pro-forma cash flow

* Follow guidelines for (5).

C. Supporting Documents

Personal financial statement (all banks have these forms)

Copy of proposed lease or purchase agreement for building space

Copy of licenses and other legal documents

Copy of resumes of all principals

Copies of letters of intent from suppliers, etc.

Writing The Business Plan - What It Includes

What goes in a business plan? This is an excellent question to ask. And, one that many new and potential small business owners should ask, but oftentimes don't ask. The body of the business plan can be divided into four distinct sections:

1) The description of the business,

2) The marketing plan,

3) The financial management plan and

4) The management plan.

Addenda to the business plan should include the executive summary, supporting documents and financial projections.

Description of the business

In this section, provide a detailed description of your business. An excellent question to ask yourself is: "What business am I in?" In answering this question include your products, market and services as well as a thorough description of what makes your business unique. Remember, however, that as you develop your business plan, you may have to modify or revise your initial questions.

The business description section is divided into three primary sections. Section 1 actually describes your business, Section 2 the product or service you will be offering and Section 3 the location of your business, and why this location is desirable.

1. Business Description

When describing your business, generally you should explain:

Legalities - business form: proprietorship, partnership, corporation, franchise. What licenses or permits you will need.

Business type: merchandising, manufacturing or service.

What your product or service is.

Is it a new independent business, a takeover, an expansion, a franchise?

Why your business will be profitable. What are the growth opportunities?

When your business will be open (days, hours).

What you have learned about your kind of business or franchise from outside sources (trade suppliers, bankers, other franchise owners, franchisor, publications).

A cover sheet goes before the description. It includes the name, address and telephone number of the business and the names of all principals. In the description of your business, describe the unique aspects and how or why they will appeal to consumers. Emphasize any special features that you feel will appeal to customers and explain how and why these features are appealing.

The description of your business should clearly identify goals and objectives and it should clarify why you are, or why you want to be, in business.

2. Product/Service

Try to describe the benefits of your goods and services from your customers' perspective.

Successful business owners know or at least have an idea of what their customers want or expect from them. This type of anticipation can be helpful in building customer satisfaction and loyalty. And, it certainly is a good strategy for beating the competition or retaining your competitiveness. Describe:

What you are selling.

How your product or service will benefit the customer.

Which products/services (in your case the franchise) are in demand; if there will be a steady flow of cash.

What is different about the product or service your franchise is offering.

3. The Location

The location of your business can play a decisive role in its success or failure. Your location should be built around your customers, it should be accessible and it should provide a sense of security. Consider these questions when addressing this section of your business plan:

What are your location needs?

What kind of space will you need?

Why is the area desirable? the building desirable?

Is it easily accessible? Is public transportation available? Is street lighting adequate?

Are market shifts or demographic shifts occurring?

It may be a good idea to make a checklist of questions you identify when developing your business plan. Categorize your questions and, as you answer each question, remove it from your list.

The Marketing Plan

Marketing plays a vital role in successful business ventures. How well you market your business, along with a few other considerations, will ultimately determine your degree of success or failure.

The key element of a successful marketing plan is to know your customers -- their likes, dislikes, expectations. By identifying these factors, you can develop a marketing strategy that will allow you to arouse and fulfill their needs.

Identify your customers by their age, sex, income/educational level and residence. At first, target only those customers who are more likely to purchase your product or service. As your customer base expands, you may need to consider modifying the marketing plan to include other customers.

Develop a marketing plan by answering these questions. Potential franchise owners will have to use the marketing strategy the franchisor has developed; however, it should be included in your business plan and contain answers to the questions outlined below.

Who are your customers? Define your target market(s).

Are your markets growing? steady? declining?

Is your franchise market share growing? steady? declining?

Has your franchisor segmented your markets?

Are your markets large enough to expand, depending on franchisor restrictions?

How will you attract, hold, increase your market share? Will the franchisor provide assistance in this area? Based on the franchisor's strategy, how will you promote your sales?

What pricing strategy, if any, has the franchisor devised?

1. Competition

Competition is a way of life. We compete for jobs, promotions, scholarships to institutes of higher learning, in sports -- and in almost every aspect of your lives. Nations compete for the consumer in the global marketplace as do individual business owners. Advances in technology can send the profit margins of a successful business into a tailspin causing them to plummet overnight or within a few hours.

When considering these and other factors, we can conclude that business is a highly competitive, volatile arena. Because of this volatility and competitiveness, it is important to know your competitors.

Questions like these can help you:

Who are your five nearest direct competitors?

Who are your indirect competitors?

How are their businesses: steady? increasing? decreasing?

What have you learned from their operations? from their advertising?

What are their strengths and weaknesses?

How does their product or service differ from yours?

Start a file on each of your competitors. Keep manila envelopes of their advertising and promotional materials and their pricing strategy techniques. Review these files periodically, determining when and how often they advertise, sponsor promotions and offer sales. Study the copy used in the advertising and promotional materials, and their sales strategy. For example, is their copy short? descriptive? catchy? or how much do they reduce prices for sales? Using this technique can help you to understand your competitors better and how they operate their businesses.

2. Pricing and Sales

Your pricing strategy is another marketing technique you can use to improve your overall competitiveness. It may be a good idea to get a feel for the pricing strategy your competitors are using. That way you can determine if your prices are in line with competitors in your market area and if they are in line with industry averages.

Some of the pricing strategies you may use, depending on the type of business, are:

Retail cost and pricing

Competitive position

Pricing below competition

Pricing above competition

Price lining

Multiple pricing

Service costs and pricing (for service businesses only)

Service components

Material costs

Labor costs

Overhead costs

The key to success is to have a well-planned strategy, to establish your policies and to constantly monitor prices and operating costs to ensure profits. It is a good policy to keep abreast of the changes in the marketplace because these changes can affect your competitiveness and profit margins.

3. Advertising and Public Relations

How you advertise and promote your business may make or break your business. Having a good product or service and not advertising and promoting it is like not having a business at all. Many business owners operate under the mistaken concept that the business will promote itself, and channel money that should be used for advertising and promotions to other areas of the business. Advertising and promotions, however, are the life line of a business and should be treated as such.

Devise a plan that uses advertising and networking as a means to promote your business. Develop short, descriptive copy (text material) that clearly identifies your goods or services, its location and price. Use catchy phrases to arouse the interest of your readers, listeners or viewers.

Make sure the advertisements you create are consistent with the image you are trying to project.

Remember the more care and attention you devote to your marketing program, the more successful your business will be.

Business Plan Outline Guide - The Management Plan

Managing a business requires more than just the desire to be your own boss. It demands dedication, persistence, the ability to make decisions and the ability to manage both employees and finances. Your management plan, along with your marketing and financial management plans, sets the foundation for and facilitates the success of your business.

Like plants and equipment, people are resources -- they are the most valuable asset a business has. You will soon discover that employees and staff will play an important role in the total operation of your business. Consequently, it's imperative that you know what skills you possess and those you lack since you will have to hire personnel to supply the skills that you lack. Additionally, it is imperative that you know how to manage and treat your employees. Make them a part of the team. Keep them informed of, and get their feedback regarding, changes. Employees oftentimes have excellent ideas that can lead to new market areas, innovations to existing products or services or new product lines or services which can improve your overall competitiveness.

Your management plan should answer questions such as:

How does your background/business experience help you in this business?

What are your weaknesses and how can you compensate for them?

Who will be on the management team?

What are their strengths/weaknesses?

What are their duties?

Are these duties clearly defined?

What are your current personnel needs?

What are your plans for hiring and training personnel?

What salaries, benefits, vacations, holidays will you offer?

What benefits, if any, can you afford at this point?

The Financial Management Plan

Sound financial management is one of the best ways for your business to remain profitable and solvent. How well you manage the finances of your business is the cornerstone of every successful business venture. Each year thousands of potentially successful businesses fail because of poor financial management. As a business owner, you will need to identify and implement policies that will lead to and ensure that you will meet your financial obligations.

To effectively manage your finances, plan a sound, realistic budget by determining the actual amount of money needed to open your business (start-up costs) and the amount needed to keep it open (operating costs). The first step to building a sound financial plan is to devise a start-up budget. Your start-up budget will usually include such one-time-only costs as major equipment, utility deposits, down payments, etc.

The start-up budget should allow for these expenses.

Start-up Budget

Personnel (costs prior to opening)

Legal/professional fees

Occupancy

Equipment

Supplies

Salaries/wages

Income

Utilities

Payroll expenses

Licenses/permits

Insurance

Advertising/promotions

Accounting

An operating budget is prepared when you are actually ready to open for business. The operating budget will reflect your priorities in terms of how your spend your money, the expenses you will incur and how you will meet those expenses (income). Your operating budget also should include money to cover the first three to six months of operation. It should allow for the following expenses.

Operating Budget

Personnel

Rent

Loan payments

Legal/accounting

Supplies

Salaries/wages

Dues/subscriptions/fees

Repairs/maintenance

Insurance

Advertising/promotions

Depreciation

Payroll expenses

Taxes

Miscellaneous expenses

The financial section of your business plan should include any loan applications you've filed, a capital equipment and supply list, balance sheet, break-even analysis, pro-forma income projections (profit and loss statement) and pro-forma cash flow. The income statement and cash flow projections should include a three-year summary, detail by month for the first year, and detail by quarter for the second and third years.

The accounting system and the inventory control system that you will be using is generally addressed in this section of the business plan also. Whether you develop the accounting and inventory systems yourself, have an outside financial advisor develop the systems, you will need to acquire a thorough understanding of each and how it operates. Your financial advisor can assist you in developing this section of your business plan.

The following questions should help you determine the amount of start-up capital you will need to purchase and open your business.

How much money do you have?

How much money will you need for start-up?

How much money will you need to stay in business?Other questions that you will need to consider are:

What type of accounting system will your use? Is it a single entry or dual entry system?

What will your sales goals and profit goals for the coming year be?

What financial projections will you need to include in your business plan?

What kind of inventory control system will you use?

Your plan should include an explanation of all projections. Unless you are thoroughly familiar with financial statements, get help in preparing your cash flow and income statements and your balance sheet. Your aim is not to become a financial wizard, but to understand the financial tools well enough to gain their benefits. Your accountant or financial advisor can help you accomplish this goal.

C. How to Attract Investors

Venture capital financing is a method used for Raising Cash For Business and Getting Investments for Business, but less popular than borrowing. Venture capital firms, like banks, supply you with the funds necessary to operate your business, but they do it differently. Banks are creditors; they expect you to repay the borrowed money. Venture capital firms are owners; they hold stock in the company, adding their invested capital to its equity base. While banks may concentrate on cash flow, venture capital firms invest for long-term capital. Commonly, these firms look for their investment to appreciate three to five times in five or seven years.

One way of explaining the different ways in which banks and venture capital firms evaluate a small business seeking funds is: Banks look at its immediate future, but are most heavily influenced by its past; venture capitalists look to its longer run future.

To be sure, venture capital firms and individuals are interested in many of the same factors that influence bankers in their analysis of loan applications from smaller companies. All financial people want to know the results and ratios of past operations, the amount and intended use of the needed funds, and the earnings and financial condition of future projections.

But venture capitalists look much more closely at the features of the product and the size of the market than do commercial banks.

What Venture Capital Firms Look For

Banks are creditors. They're interested in the product/market position of the company for assurance that this product or service can provide steady sales and generate sufficient cash flow to repay the loan. They look at projections to be certain that owners/managers have done their homework.

Venture capital firms are owners. They hold stock in the company, adding their invested capital to its equity base. Therefore, they examine existing or planned products or services and the potential markets for them with extreme care. They invest only in firms they believe can rapidly increase sales and generate substantial profits. The reason for this is that venture capital firms invest for long-term capital, not for interest income. A common estimate is that they look for three to five times their investment in five or seven years.

Of course, venture capitalists don't realize capital gains on all their investments. Certainly they don't make capital gains of 300 to 500% except on a very limited portion of their total investments. But their intent is to find venture projects with this appreciation potential to make up for investments that aren't successful.

Venture capital is risky due to the difficulty of judging the worth of a business in its early stages. Therefore, most venture capital firms set rigorous policies for venture proposal size, maturity of the seeking company, management of the seeking company, and "something special" in the plan that is submitted. They also have rigorous evaluation procedures to reduce risks, since their investments are unprotected in the event of failure.

Size of the Venture Proposal

Most venture capital firms are interested in investment projects requiring an investment of $250,000 to $1,500,000. Projects requiring under $250,000 are of limited interest because of the high cost of investigation and administration; however, some venture capital firms will consider smaller proposals if the investment is intriguing enough.

The typical venture capital firm receives over 400 proposals a year. Probably 90% of these will be rejected quickly because they don't fit the established geographical, technical or market area policies of the firm - or because they have been poorly prepared.

The remaining 10% are carefully investigated. These investigations are expensive. Firms may hire consultants to evaluate the product, particularly when it is the result of innovation or is technologically complex. The market size and competitive position of the company are analyzed by contacts with present and potential customers, suppliers, and others. Production costs are reviewed. The financial condition of the company is confirmed by an auditor. The legal form and registration of the business are checked. Most importantly, the character and competence of the management are evaluated by the venture capital firm, normally via a thorough background check.

These preliminary investigations may cost a venture firm between $2,000 and $3,000 per company investigated. They result in perhaps ten to fifteen proposals of interest. Then, second investigations, more thorough and more expensive than the first, reduce the number of proposals under consideration to only three or four. Eventually, the firm invests in one or two of these.

Most venture capital firms' investment interest is limited to projects proposed by companies with some operating history, even though they may not yet have shown a profit. Companies that can expand into a new product line or a new market with additional funds are particularly interesting. The venture capital firm can provide funds to enable such companies to grow in a spurt rather than gradually as they would on retained earnings. Raising Money From Investors.

Companies that are just starting or that have serious financial difficulties may interest some venture capitalists, if the potential for significant gain over the long run can be identified and assessed. If the venture firm has already extended its portfolio to a large risk concentration, they may be reluctant to invest in these areas because of increased risk of loss.

Although most venture capital firms will not consider a great many proposals from start-up companies, there are a small number of venture firms that will do "start-up" financing. The small firm that has a well thought-out plan and can demonstrate that its management group has an outstanding record (even if it is with other companies) has a decided edge in acquiring this kind of seed capital.

Most venture capital firms concentrate primarily on the competence and character of the management. They feel that even mediocre products can be successfully manufactured, promoted, and distributed by an experienced, energetic management group.

They look for a group that is able to work together easily and productively, especially under conditions of stress from temporary reversals and competition problems. Obviously, analysis of managerial skill is difficult. A partner or senior executive of a venture capital firm normally spends at least a week at the offices of a company being considered, talking with and observing the management to estimate their competence and character.

Venture capital firms usually require that the company under consideration have a complete management group. Each of the important functional areas product design, marketing, production, finance, and control - must be under the direction of a trained, experienced member of the group. Responsibilities must be clearly assigned. And, in addition to a thorough understanding of the industry, each member of the management team must be firmly committed to the company and its future.

Next in importance to the excellence of the management group, most venture capital firms seek a distinctive element in the strategy or product/market/process position of the company. This distinctive element may be a new feature of the product or process or a particular skill or technical competence of the management. But it must exist. It must provide a competitive advantage.

Elements of a Venture Proposal
Purpose and Objectives
Include a summary of the what and why of the project.

Proposed Financing: You must state the amount of money you will need from the beginning to the maturity of the project proposed, how the proceeds will be used, how you plan to structure the financing, and why the amount designated is required.

Marketing: Describe the market segment you've got or plan to get, the competition, the characteristics of the market, and your plans (with costs) for getting or holding the market segment you're aiming at.

History of the Firm: Summarize the significant financial and organizational milestones,

Description of employees and employee relations, explanations of banking relationships, recounting of major services or products your firm has offered during its existence, and the like.

Description of the Product or Service: Include a full description of the product (process) or service offered by the firm and the costs associated with it in detail.

Financial Statements: Include statements for both the past few years and pro forma projections (balance sheets, income statements, and cash flows) for the next three to five years, showing the effect anticipated if the project is undertaken and if the financing is secured. (This should include an analysis of key variables affecting financial performance, showing what could happen if the projected level of revenue is not attained.)

Capitalization: Provide a list of shareholders, how much is invested to date, and in what form (equity/debt).

Biographical Sketches: Describe the work histories and qualifications of key owners and employees.

Principal Suppliers and Customers, Problems Anticipated and Other Pertinent Information

Provide a candid discussion of any contingent liabilities, pending litigation, tax or patent difficulties, and any other contingencies that might affect the project you're proposing. List the names, addresses and the

Telephone numbers of suppliers and customers; they will be contacted to verify your statement about payments (suppliers) and products (customers).

Provisions of the Investment Proposal

What happens when, after the exhaustive investigation and analysis, the venture capital firms decides to invest in a company? Most venture firms prepare an equity financing proposal that details the amount of money to be provided, the percentage of common stock to be surrendered in exchange for these funds, the interim financing method to be used and the protective covenants to be included.

This proposal will be discussed with the management of the company. The final financing agreement will be negotiated and generally represents a compromise between the management of the company and the partners or senior executives of the venture capital firm. The important elements of this compromise are: ownership, control, annual charges, and final objectives.

Ownership

Venture capital financing is not inexpensive for the owners of a small business. The partners of the venture firm buy a portion of the business' equity in exchange for their investment.

This percentage of equity varies, of course, and depends on the amount of money provided, the success and worth of the business, and the anticipated investment return. It can range from perhaps 10% in the case of an established, profitable company to as much as 80 or 90% for beginning or financially troubled firms.

Most venture capital firms, at least initially, don't want a position of more than 30 to 40% because they want the owner to have the incentive to keep building the business. If additional financing is required to support

Business growth, the outsiders' stake may exceed 50% but investors realize that small business owner/managers can lose their entrepreneurial zeal under those circumstances. In the final analysis, however, the venture firm, regardless of its percentage of ownership, really wants to leave control in the hands of the company's managers because it is really investing in that management team in the first place.

Most venture firms determine the ratio of funds provided to equity requested by a comparison of the present financial worth of the contributions made by each of the parties to the agreement. The present value of the contribution by the owner of a starting or financially troubled company is obviously rated low. Often it is estimated as just the existing value of his or her idea and the competitive costs of the owner's time. The contribution by the owners of a thriving business is valued much higher. Generally, it is capitalized at a multiple of the current earnings and/or net worth.

Financial valuation is not an exact science. The final compromise on the worth of the owner's contribution in the equity financing agreement is likely to be much lower than the owner thinks it should be and considerably higher than the partners of the capital firm think it might be. In the ideal situation, of course, the two parties to the agreement are able to do together what neither could do separately: 1) the company is able to grow fast enough with the additional funds to do more than overcome the owner's loss of equity; and 2) the investment grows at a sufficient rate to compensate the venture capitalists for assuming the risk.

An equity financing agreement with an outcome in five to seven years which pleases both parties is ideal. Since the parties cannot see this outcome in the present, neither will be perfectly satisfied with the compromise reached.

It is important, though, for the business owner to look at the future. He or she should carefully consider the impact of the ratio of funds invested to the ownership given up, not only for the present, but for the years to come.

Control

Control is a much simpler issue to resolve. Unlike the division of ownership over which the venture firm and management are likely to disagree, control is an issue in which they have a common interest. While it is understandable that the management of a small company will have some anxiety in this area, the partners of a venture firm have little interest in assuming control of the business. They have neither the technical nor the managerial personnel to run a number of small companies in diverse industries. They much prefer to leave operating control to the existing management.

The venture capital firm does, however, want to participate in any strategic decisions that might change the basic product/market character of the company and in any major investment decisions that might divert or deplete the financial resources of the company. They will, therefore, generally ask that at least one partner be made a director of the company.

They also want to be able to assume control and attempt to rescue their investment if severe financial, operating or marketing problems

Develop. Thus, they will usually include protective covenants in their equity financing agreements to permit them to take control and appoint new officers if financial performance is very poor.

Annual Charges

The investment of the venture capital firm may be in the final form of direct stock ownership which does not impose fixed charges. More likely, it will be in an interim form - convertible subordinated debentures or preferred stock. Financings may also be straight loans with options or warrants that can be converted to a future equity position at a pre-established price.

The convertible debenture form of financing is like a loan. The debentures can be converted at an established ratio to the common stock of the company within a given period, so that the venture capital firm can prepare to realize their capital gains at their option in the future. These instruments are often subordinated to existing and planned debt to permit the company invested in to obtain additional bank financing.

Debentures also provide additional security and control for the venture firm and impose a fixed charge for interest (and possibly principal) on the company. The owner/manager of a small company seeking equity financing should consider the burden of any fixed annual charges resulting from the financing agreement.

Final Objectives

Venture capital firms generally intend to realize capital gains on their investments by providing for a stock buy-back by the small firm, by arranging a public offering of stock of the company invested in or by providing for a merger with a larger firm that has publicly traded stock. They usually hope to do this within five to seven years of their initial investment. (It should be noted that several additional stages of financing may be required over this period of time.)

Most equity financing agreements include provisions guaranteeing that the venture capital firm may participate in any stock sale or approve any merger, regardless of their percentage of stock ownership. Sometimes the agreement will require that the management work toward an eventual stock sale or merger. Clearly, the owner/manager of a small company seeking equity financing must consider the future impact upon his or her own stock holdings and personal ambition of the venture firm's aims, since taking in a venture capitalist as a partner may be virtually a commitment to eventually sell out or go public.

Types of Venture Capital Firms

Traditional Partnerships are often established by wealthy families to aggressively manage a portion of their funds by investing in small companies.

Professionally Managed Pools are made up of institutional money and which operate like the traditional partnerships.

Investment Banking Firms usually trade in more established securities, but occasionally form investor syndicates for venture proposals.

Insurance Companies often have required a portion of equity as a condition of their loans to smaller companies as protection against inflation.

Manufacturing Companies have sometimes looked upon investing in smaller companies as a means of supplementing their research and development programs.

In addition to these venture capital firms, there are individual private investors and finders. Finders, which can be firms or individuals, often know the capital industry and may be able to help the small company seeking capital to locate it, though they are generally not sources of capital themselves. Care should be exercised so that a small business owner deals with reputable, professional finders whose fees are in line with industry practice. Further, it should be noted that venture capitalists generally prefer working directly with principals in making investments, though finders may provide useful introductions.

The Importance of Formal Financial Planning

In case there is any doubt about the implications of the previous sections, it should be noted that it is extremely difficult for any small firm especially the starting or struggling company - to get venture capital.

There is one thing, however, that owner/managers of small businesses can do to improve the chances of their venture proposals at least escaping the 90% which are almost immediately rejected. In a word - plan.

Having financial plans demonstrates to venture capital firms that you are a competent manager, that you may have that special managerial edge over other small business owners looking for equity money. You may gain a decided advantage through well-prepared plans and projections that include: cash budgets, pro forma statements, and capital investment analysis and capital source studies.

Cash budgets should be projected for one year and prepared monthly.

They should combine expected sales revenues, cash receipts, material, labor and overhead expenses, and cash disbursements on a monthly basis. This permits anticipation of fluctuations in the level of cash and planning for short term borrowing and investment.

Pro forma statements should be prepared for planning up to three years ahead. They should include both income statements and balance sheets.

Again, these should be prepared quarterly to combine expected sales revenues; production, marketing and administrative expenses; profits; product, market or process investments; and supplier, bank or investment company borrowings. Pro forma statements permit you to anticipate the financial results of your operations and to plan intermediate term borrowings and investments.

Capital investment analyses and capital source studies should be prepared for planning up to five years ahead. The investment analyses should compare rate of return for product, market, or process investment, while the source alternatives should compare the cost and availability of debt and equity and the expected level of retained earnings, which together will support the selected investments. These analyses and source studies should be prepared quarterly so you may anticipate the financial consequences of changes in your company's strategy. They will allow you to plan long term borrowings, equity placements, and major investments.

There is a bonus in making such projections. They force you to consider the results of your actions. Your estimates must be explicit; you have to examine and evaluate your managerial records; disagreements must be resolved - or at least discussed and understood. Financial planning may be burdensome but it is one of the keys to business success.

Now, making these financial plans will not guarantee that you'll be able to get venture capital. Not making them will virtually assure that you won't receive favorable consideration from venture capitalists.

D. How to Obtain Business Loans the Easy Way

Some businesspersons cannot understand why a lending institution refused to lend them money. Others have no trouble getting funds, but are surprised to find strings attached to their loans. Such owner-managers fail to realize that banks and other lenders have to operate by certain principles just as do other types of business.

This Guide discusses the following fundamentals of borrowing: (1) credit worthiness, (2) kinds of loans, (3) amount of money needed, (4) collateral, (5) loan restrictions and limitation, (6) the loan application, and (7) standards which the lender uses to evaluate the application.

Introduction

Inexperience with borrowing procedures often created resentment and bitterness. The stories of three businesspersons illustrate this point.

"I'll never trade here again," Bill Smith said when his bank refused to grant him a loan. "I'd like to let you have it, Bill," the banker said, "but your firm isn't earning enough to meet your current obligations." Mr. Smith was unaware of a vital financial fact, namely, that lending institutions have to be certain that the borrower's business can repay the loan.

Tom Jones lost his temper when the bank refused him a loan because he did not know what kind of or how much money he needed. "We hesitate to lend," the banker said, "to business owners with such vague ideas of what and how much they need."

John William's' case was somewhat different. He didn't explode until after he got the loan. When the papers were ready to sign, he realized that the loan agreement put certain limitations on his business activities. "You can't dictate to me," he said and walked out of the bank. What he didn't realize was that the limitations were for his good as well as for the bank's protection.

Knowledge of the financial facts of business life could have saved all three the embarrassment of losing their tempers. Even more important, such information would have helped them to borrow money at a time when their businesses needed it badly.

This Guide is designed to give the highlights of what is involved in sound business borrowing. It should be helpful to those who have little or no experience with borrowing. More experienced owner-managers should find it useful in re-evaluating their borrowing operations.

Is Your Firm Credit Worthy?

The ability to obtain money when you need it is as necessary to the operation of your business as is a good location or the right equipment, reliable sources of supplies and materials, or an adequate labor force. Before a bank or any other lending agency will lend you money, the loan officer must feel satisfied with the answers to the five following questions:

1. What sort of person are you, the prospective borrower? By all odds, the character of the borrower comes first. Next is your ability to manage your business.

2. What are you going to do with the money? The answer to this question will determine the type of loan, short or long-term. Money to be used for the purchase of seasonal inventory will require quicker repayment than money used to buy fixed assets.

3. When and how do you plan to pay it back? Your banker's judgment of your business ability and the type of loan will be a deciding factor in the answer to this question.

4. Is the cushion in the loan large enough? In other words, does the amount requested make suitable allowance for unexpected developments? The banker decides this question on the basis of your financial statement which sets forth the condition of your business and on the collateral pledged.

5. What is the outlook for business in general and for your business particularly?

Adequate Financial Data Is a "Must"

The banker wants to make loans to businesses which are solvent, profitable, and growing. The two basic financial statements used to determine those conditions are the balance sheet and profit-and-loss statement. The former is the major yardstick for solvency and the latter for profits. A continuous series of these two statements over a period of time is the principal device for measuring financial stability and growth potential.

In interviewing loan applicants and in studying their records the banker is especially interested in the following facts and figures.

General Information: Are the books and records up-to-date and in good condition? What is the condition of accounts payable? Of notes payable? What are the salaries of the owner-manager and other company officers? Are all taxes being paid currently? what is the order backlog? What is the insurance coverage?

Accounts Receivable: Are there indications that some of the accounts receivable have already been pledged to another creditor? What is the accounts receivable turnover? Is the accounts receivable total weakened because many customers are far behind in their payments? Has a large enough reserve been set up to cover doubtfull accounts? How much do the largest accounts owe and what percentage of your total accounts does this amount represent?

Inventories: Is merchandise in good shape or will it have to be marked down? How much raw material is on hand? How much work is in process? How much of the inventory is finished goods?

Is there any obsolete inventory? Has an excessive amount of inventory been consigned to customers? Is inventory turnover in line with the turnover for other businesses in the same industry? Or is money being tied up too long in inventory?

Fixed Assets: What is the type, age, and condition of the equipment? What are the depreciation policies? What are the details of mortgages or conditional sales contracts? What are the future acquisition plans?

What Kind Of Money?

When you set out to borrow money for your firm, it is important to know the kind of money you need from a bank or other lending institution. There are three kinds of money: short term, term money, and equity capital.

Keep in mind that the purpose for which the funds are to be used is an important factor in deciding the kind of money needed. But even so, deciding what kind of money to use is not always easy. It is sometimes complicated by the fact that you may be using some of the various kinds of money at the same time and for identical purposes.

Keep in mind that a very important distinction between the types of money is the source of repayment. Generally short-term loans are repaid from the liquidation of current assets which they have financed. Long-term loans are usually repaid from earnings.

Short-Term Bank Loans

You can use short-term bank loans for purposes such as financing accounts receivable for, say 30 to 60 days. Or you can use them for purposes that take longer to pay off - such as for building a seasonal inventory over a period of 5 to 6 months. Usually, lenders expect short-term loans to be repaid after their purposes have been served: for example, accounts receivable loans, when the outstanding accounts have been paid by the borrower's customers, and inventory loans, when the inventory has been converted into salable merchandise.

Banks grant such money either on your general credit reputation with an unsecured loan or on a secured loan.

The unsecured loan is the most frequently used form of bank credit for short term purposes. You do not have to put up collateral because the bank relies on your credit reputation.

The secured loan involves a pledge of some or all of your assets. The bank requires security as a protection for its depositors against the risks that are involved even in business situations where the chances of success are good.

Term Borrowing

Term borrowing provides money you plan to pay back over a fairly long time. Some people break it down into two forms: (1) intermediate - loans longer than 1 year but less than 5 years, and (2) long-term - loan for more than 5 years.

However, for your purpose of matching the kind of money to the needs of your company, think of term borrowing as a kind of money which you probably will pay back in periodic installments from earnings.

Equity Capital

Some people confuse term borrowing and equity (or investment) capital. Yet there is a big difference. You don't have to repay equity money. It is money you get by selling a part interest in your business.

You take people into your company who are willing to risk their money in it. They are interested in potential income rather than in an immediate return on their investment.

How Much Money?

The amount of money you need to borrow depends on the purpose for which you need funds. Figuring the amount of money required for business construction, conversion, or expansion - term loans or equity capital - is relatively easy. Equipment manufacturers, architects, and builders will readily supply you with cost estimates.

On the other hand, the amount of working capital you need depends upon the type of business you're in. While rule-of-thumb ratios may be helpful as a starting point, a detailed projection of sources and uses of funds over some future period of time - usually for 12 months - is a better approach.

In this way, the characteristics of the particular situation can be taken into account. Such a projection is developed through the combination of a predicted budget and a cash forecast.

The budget is based on recent operating experience plus your best judgment of performance during the coming period. The cash forecast is your estimates of cash receipts and disbursements during the budget period. Thus, the budget and the cash forecast together represent your plan for meeting your working capital requirements.

To plan your working capital requirements, it is important to know the "cash flow" which your business will generate. This involves simply a consideration of all elements of cash receipts and disbursements at the time they occur. These elements are listed in the profit-and-loss statement which has been adapted to show cash flow. They should be projected for each month.

What Kind of Collateral?

Sometimes, your signature is the only security the bank needs when making a loan. At other times, the bank requires additional assurance that the money will be repaid. The kind and amount of security depends on the bank and on the borrower's situation.

If the loan required cannot be justified by the borrower's financial statements alone, a pledge of security may bridge the gap. The types of security are: endorsers; co-makers and guarantors; assignment of leases; trust receipts and floor planning; chattel mortgages; real estate; accounts receivables; saving accounts; life insurance policies; and stocks and bonds. In a substantial number of States where the Uniform Commercial Code has been enacted, paperwork for recording loan transactions will be greatly simplified.

Endorsers, Co-makers, and Guarantors

Borrowers often get other people to sign a note in order to bolster their own credit.

These endorsers are contingently liable for the note they sign. If the borrower fails to pay up, the bank expects the endorser to make the note good. Sometimes, the endorser may be asked to pledge assets or securities too.

A co-maker is one who creates an obligation jointly with the borrower. In such cases, bank can collect directly from either the maker or the co-maker.

A guarantor is one who guarantees the payment of a note by signing a guaranty commitment. Both private and government lenders often require guarantees from offices of corporations in order to assure continuity of effective management. Sometimes, a manufacturer will act as guarantor for customers.

Assignment of Leases

The assigned lease as security is similar to the guarantee. It is used, for example, in some franchise situations.

The bank lends the money on a building and takes a mortgage. Then the lease, which the dealer and the parent franchise company work out, is assigned so that the bank automatically receives the rent payments. In this manner, the bank is guaranteed repayment of the loan.

Warehouse Receipts

Banks also take commodities as security by lending money on a warehouse receipt. Such a receipt is usually delivered directly to the bank and shows that the merchandise used as security either has been placed in a public warehouse or has been left on your premises under the control of one of your employees who is bonded (as in field warehousing). Such loans are generally made on staple or standard merchandise which can be readily marketed. The typical warehouse receipt loan is for a percentage of the estimated value of the goods used as security.

Trust Receipts and Floor Planning

Merchandise, such as automobiles, appliances, and boats, has to be displayed to be sold. The only way many small marketers can afford such displays is by borrowing money. Such loans are often secured by a note and a trust receipt.

This trust receipt is the legal paper for floor planning. It is used for serial-numbered merchandise. When you sign one, you (1) acknowledge receipt of the merchandise, (2) agree to keep the merchandise in trust for the bank, and (3) promise to pay the bank as you sell the goods.

Chattel Mortgages

If you buy equipment such as a cash register or a delivery truck, you may want to get a chattel mortgage loan. You give the bank a lien on the equipment you are buying.

The bank also evaluates the present and future market value of the equipment being used to secure the loan. How rapidly will it depreciate? Does the borrower have the necessary fire, theft, property damage, and public liability insurance on the equipment? The banker has to be sure that the borrower protects the equipment.

Real Estate

Real estate is another form of collateral for long-term loans. When taking a real estate mortgage, the bank finds out: (1) the location of the real estate, (2) its physical condition, (3) its foreclosure value, and (4) the amount of insurance carried on the property.

Accounts Receivable

Many banks lend money on accounts receivable. In effect, you are counting on your customers to pay your note.

The bank may take accounts receivable on a notification or a non-notification plan.

Under the notification plan, the purchaser of the goods is informed by the bank that his or her account has been assigned to it and he or she is asked to pay the bank. Under the non-notification plan, the borrower's customers continue to pay you the sums due on their accounts and you pay the bank.

Savings Accounts

Sometimes, you might get a loan by assigning to the bank a savings account. In such cases, the bank gets an assignment from you and keeps your passbook. If you assign an account in another bank as collateral, the lending bank asks the other bank to mark its records to show that the account is held as collateral.

Life Insurance

Another kind of collateral is life insurance. Banks will lend up to the cash value of a life insurance policy. You have to assign the policy to the bank.

If the policy is on the life of an executive of a small corporation, corporate resolutions must be made authorizing the assignment. Most insurance companies allow you to sign the policy back to the original beneficiary when the assignment to the bank ends.

Some people like to use life insurance as collateral rather than borrow directly from insurance companies. One reason is that a bank loan is often more convenient to obtain and usually may be obtained at a lower interest rate.

Stocks and Bonds

If you use stocks and bonds as collateral, they must be marketable. As a protection against market declines and possible expenses of liquidation, banks usually lend no more than 75 percent of the market value of high grade stock. On Federal Government or municipal bonds, they may be willing to lend 90 percent or more of their market value.

The bank may ask the borrower for additional security or payment whenever the market value of the stocks or bonds drops below the bank's required margin.

What Are the Lender's Rules?

Lending institutions are not interested in loan repayments. They are interested in borrowers with healthy profit-making businesses.

Therefore, whether or not collateral is required for a loan, they set loan limitation and restrictions to protect themselves against unnecessary risks and at the same time against poor management practices by their borrowers. Often some owner-managers consider loan limitations a burden.

Yet others feel that such limitation also offer an opportunity for improving their management techniques.

Especially in making long-term loans, the borrower as well as the lender should be thinking of: (1) the net earning power of the borrowing company, (2) the capability of its management, (3) the long range prospects of the company, and (4) the long range prospects of the industry of which the company is a part. Such factors often mean that limitation increase as the duration of the loan increases.

What Kinds of Limitation?

The kinds of limitations, which an owner-manager finds set upon the company depends, to a great extent, on the company. If the company is a good risk, only minimum limitations need be set. A poor risk, of course, is different. Its limitation should be greater than those of a stronger company.

Look now for a few moments at the kinds of limitations and restrictions which the lender may set. Knowing what they are can help you see how they affect your operations.

The limitations which you will usually run into when you borrow money are:

(1) Repayment terms.

(2) Pledging or the use of security.

(3) Periodic reporting.

A loan agreement, as you may already know, is a tailor-made document covering, or referring to, all the terms and conditions of the loan.

With it, the lender does two things: (1) protects position as a creditor (keeps that position in as protected a state as it was on the date the loan was made) and (2) assures repayment according to the terms.

The lender reasons that the borrower's business should generate enough funds to repay the loan while taking care of other needs. The lender considers that cash inflow should be great enough to do this without hurting the working capital of the borrower.

Covenants - Negative and Positive

The actual restrictions in a loan agreement come under a section known as covenants. Negative covenants are things which the borrower may not do without prior approval from the lender. Some examples are: further additions to the borrower's total debt, non-pledge to others of the borrower's assets and issuance of dividends in excess of the terms of the loan agreement

On the other hand, positive covenants spell out things which the borrower must do. Some examples are: (1) maintenance of a minimum net working capital, (2) carrying of adequate insurance, (3) repaying the loan according to the terms of the agreement, and (4) supplying the lender with financial statements and reports.

Overall, however, loan agreements may be amended from time to time and exceptions made. Certain provisions may be waived from one year to the next with the consent of the lender.

You Can Negotiate

Next time you go to borrow money, thrash out the lending terms before you sign. It is good practice no matter how badly you may need the money.

Ask to see the papers in advance of the loan closing. Legitimate lenders are glad to cooperate.

Chances are that the lender may "give" some on the terms. Keep in mind also that, while your are mulling over the terms, you may want to get the advice of your associates and outside advisors.

In short, try to get terms which you know your company can live with. Remember, however that once the terms have been agreed upon and the loan is made you are bound by them.

The Loan Application

Now that you have read about the various aspects of the lending process and are ready to apply for a loan. Banks and other private lending institutions, require a loan application on which you list certain information about your business

Evaluating the Application

Once you have supplied the necessary information, the next step in the borrowing process is the evaluation of your application. The officer considers this kind of thing when determining whether to grant or refuse the loan:

(1) The borrower's debt paying record to suppliers, banks, home mortgage holders, and other creditors.

(2) The ratio of the borrower's debt to net worth.

(3) The past earnings of the company.

(4) The value and conditions of the collateral which the borrower offers for security.

E. How to Effectively Manage Your Loans

Poor management is the reason why some owner-managers have trouble when they try to borrow. Those managers often fail to forecast and to plan for cash needs. The resulting business ailment is a "cash crisis."

Sound management must be practiced if loans are to be obtained and used profitably. Such management included: knowing the firm's cash flow, forecasting cash needs, planning to borrow at the appropriate time, and substantiating the firm's payback ability.

This Guide includes examples of the following: a cash budget forecast, a projection of borrowing requirements, and a cash flow schedule for repaying a loan.

In spite of respectable sales volumes, many owners of businesses run into financial trouble. Some get in so deep that they are barely able to pull their heads back above water. Others find themselves only weeks or months away from tacking "out of business" signs on their doors.

Often these owner-managers have three things in common. First, they know their line of business. Their technical ability is first rate. Second, they are poor managers. In many instances, they fail to plan ahead because of their enthusiasm for the operating side of their business. In the third place, most of them feel that additional money will solve their problems. They think that a loan will pull them out of the red.

Lending Officer's Viewpoint

Often a bank lending officer refuses or "declines" that loan request of such manager-owners. It is not that a banker lacks appreciation for the hard work and long hours which these owners put into their businesses. Nor does the bank question their good intentions.

Foremost in the lender's mind is the question: Can the firm pay back the loan? Thus, in many cases, the lender refuses the loan because the owner-manager hastily and haphazardly prepared the loan application under pressuring circumstances. As a result, the lending officer detects an air of instability and lack of planning in the owner-manager's description of his or her affairs. "How is the borrower really going to repay," the lending officer asks, "if the borrower doesn't actually know how much money is needed and how it is going to be used?"

If your request for a loan is turned down, the best bet is to accept the refusal gracefully and look for weaknesses in the presentation, You can correct these weaknesses when applying for a loan in the future.

Pertinent Questions

The lender needs the answers to several pertinent questions to determine whether or not the borrower can repay the loan. One of these questions is: What does the borrower intend to use the money for?

What Kind of Money? When you consider borrowing determine what kind of money you need. A business uses four basic types of money in its operations. Your purpose in borrowing will determine the type.

1. **Trade Credit.** This type of "money" is not borrowed. It is money you owe your suppliers who permit you to carry your fast-moving inventory on open account. A good credit experience is proven evidence of your ability to repay borrowed funds.

2. **Short-Term Credit.** Banks and other lenders will provide this type of money to carry you in your purchases of inventory for special reasons, such as buying inventory for the next selling season. Such loans are self-liquidating because they generate sales dollars. You repay short-term credit in less than a year.

3. **Long-Term Credit.** Such loans - for more than a year - are used for expansion or modernization of your business. They are repaid out of accumulated profits. Usually, the evidence of this type of loan in a business is a mortgage or a promissory note with terms.

4. **Equity Funds.** This type of money is never repaid. You get it by relinquishing a part of your profits to an investor. That is you sell an interest in your business.

Many owner-managers fail to recognize the difference between the four types of money. You should keep in mind that money borrowed for a temporary purpose should be used in the profit producing areas of your business and will be repaid out of that operation. Equity funds are those which remain in the business and increase the net worth for the owner.

Are Your Sales Adequate? Are you asking for a loan to bolster sagging sales volume? To buy additional stocks of high-volume merchandise which you feel has even greater potential? To create a new image by an over-all advertising campaign?

What Is Your Receivables Position? Are your accounts going uncollected and getting old? In effect, do you really need money to carry old accounts?

Is Your Profit Margin Adequate? Are you doing a lot of business and showing a lack of profit thus indicating that expenses are not controlled? Or is your market insufficient? What is your break-even point for profits?

What Is Your Plan For Repayment? Do you forecast your cash income and expenditures realistically?

The lender scrutinizes the cash flow of the business to determine whether or not the owner-manager is providing sufficient cash to meet the firm's obligations. The lender also has to make sure that cash needed for working capital is not being absorbed by the business into other areas of equity and thereby reducing liquidity.

The "Cash Crisis"

The experience of counselors is that all too often the business owner feels that his or her needs are financial when they are actually managerial. In such firms, money can ease the pressure temporarily, but further indebtedness only intensifies the basic problem. Money alone cannot provide the sound management needed to continue the business.

Counselors to business owners are continually faced with the "cash crisis" problem. This cash deficiency results from the lack of planning.

A mistake many purchasers of a business make is that they buy something beyond their means. They take possession of a business of some value but without one important asset - sufficient operating cash. When a buyer does not put aside working capital (cash), he or she cannot pay current bills and the rest of the story is easy to foretell.

It is the "cash crisis."

Sound management consists of arranging matters so that current liabilities are provided for as they become due and hence paid promptly. When such coordination is not present, the result is a constant "cash crisis."

Without a floating supply of cash, a business will experience occasional convulsions which distort, confuse, embarrass, and alarm everyone concerned with the enterprise. The owner-manager's employees and suppliers are the first to sense the nervousness of the situation. When they do, they begin to consider their futures in the light of these emergencies.

Lack of cash can drive a firm into bankruptcy even though its products are first rate and its operations are profitable.

Avoid A "Cash Crisis"

To avoid a "cash crisis" you should determine how much cash your firm needs for its normal operations. Then plan your finances to achieve the goal.

The amount of cash which a business will need differs because all businesses are not alike. Usually, for comfort, five to ten percent of a firm's working capital should be in cash.

In a sense, financial planning is what you anticipate your financial statements will show on a specific date and how you intend to get there. A cash forecast will indicate whether or not your plan of operation is feasible. A budget will indicate the availability of cash at all points of operations.

Cash Budgeting

When the subject of budgeting comes up, some owner-managers say, "That's for the big fellow. I know what my volume is and my bank account tells me how much money I have." These owners fail to realize that budgeting can help to eliminate errors of judgment made in haste or made on assumptions rather than facts.

The first thing you must know in budgeting is what your anticipated expenses are going to be for the period being budgeted. Then how much in sales must be generated to pay these expenses? What will be left? You must try to determine the high and low points in your operations in order to provide the adequate amount of cash. A sales analysis of previous periods will indicate when the high and low points occur.

This forecasting helps you to plan for financing the purchase of inventory and for carrying your accounts receivable. Controlling inventory and accounts receivable can help to take the strain off of your working capital.

Uses of a Cash Budget

The cash budget is the most effective tool for planning the cash requirements and resources of your business. With it you plan your financial operations - the cash you expect to take in and pay out. Your goal in budgeting is to maintain a satisfactory cash position for any contingency. When used to project the cash flow of the business, the cash budget will:

Provide efficient use of cash by timing cash disbursements to coincide with cash receipts. These actions may reduce the need for borrowing temporary additional working capital.

Point up cash deficiency periods so that predetermined borrowing requirements may be established and actual amounts determined to reduce excessive indebtedness.

Determine periods for repayment of borrowings.

establish the practicability of taking trade discounts or not taking them.

Determine periods of surplus cash for investment or purchase of inventory and equipment.

Indicate the adequacy or need for additional permanent working capital in the business.

Be Factual

The important thing to keep in mind in making a cash budget is the word "cash." Be as factual as you can. Try not to over-estimate sales or under-estimate expenses. Your sales forecast must be as accurate as possible because it is the basis for figuring your cash and expenses.

Use your experience to determine your cash sales. In seasonal businesses and those which have high-ticket merchandise, the percent of sales that are for cash will vary from month to month if they apply to your business.

A format such as that shown in the example below can help you to be factual. This example of a cash budget forecast uses two columns for each month. The second column allows you to insert the actual figures as they occur and helps in correcting mistakes for future forecasts.

Sound Management - Success Story

With sound management a firm can often achieve a goal by borrowing only a nominal amount. The experience of two partners in a Southeast business provides an example.

They obtained a contract to manufacture and install kitchen cabinets for a large builder. The contract called for installation in 4 months. To meet this deadline, the partners figured that they needed $56,500 in extra working capital.

Because this amount was more than they wanted to borrow, they asked for help from a counselor. The counselor helped the partners to come up with a borrowing requirement of only $16,000. This solution was arrived at by:

Arranging with their supplier to ship and bill for the materials monthly over a 3-month period.

Contracting with the builder to make an initial payment and 4 monthly payments.

Agreeing not to take any drawings from the business until the cash flow forecast indicated it was free and available.

Based on these facts, the partners estimated that during the 5 months (July through November) the firm should take in $88,000, pay out $56,500, and have a balance of $31,500 at the end of November. However, the problem was in July and August when expenses would run far ahead of the firm's income. To determine how a loan of $16,000 (including interest) could see the firm through these months, the following estimates were made:

**Estimate of Borrowing Requirements
To Take On Additional Contract**

	July	Aug.	Sep	Oct.	Nov.
Cash Requirements					
Inventory	15,000	10,000	7,000		
Operating Expenses	4,000	6,000	6,000	4,000	2,000
Extra Equipment	2,500				
Total	21,500	16,000	13,000	4,000	2,000
Cash Available					
Cash on Hand	2,000			2,000	18,000
Collections	10,000	10,000	15,000	20,000	31,000
Total	12,000	10,000	15,000	22,000	49,000
Excess Cash Over Receipts	0	0	2,000	18,000	47,000
Additional Cash Required	9,500	6,000	0	0	0

According to these estimates, at the end of November the partners would have cash on hand amounting to $47,000. Certain obligations would be outstanding against this cash. The first one would be the repayment of the loan of $16,000. Other obligations would be those which the partners planned to accumulate during the early months of the contract when cash on hand was at a premium, such as reserve for taxes and the partners' draw.

These estimates convinced the partners that they could perform the contract if they could get a loan. The next step was to convince the bank that their plan was sound.

For the bank lending officer's benefit, as well as their own, the partners projected the loan funds through a cash flow plan for the entire business. The cash flow schedule that was prepared is shown below. It showed: (1) that the amount of money requested would be adequate for the firm's needs and (2) the margin of cash that was expected to be available both during the contract and at the end of the contract.

Keep in mind that records are a reflection of the quality of a firm's management. Nobody knows this fact better or uses it more often than a banker.

The efficiency of an owner-manager portrays itself on the profit and loss statement (income statement). The P&L of an effective operation will show adequate profits for the particular line of business. Sales, promotion, expense control, merchandise turnover, and net profit application are the points on which you will be judged.

To determine trends, the lender looks at your current financial statement and those for the past several years. The current statement also shows the lender the makeup of your net worth.

VEGETABLE BUSINESS PLAN TEMPLATE

Cash Budget Forecast

	January Est.	Actual	February Est.	Actual
1. Cash in Bank (Start of Month)	1,400	1,400*	1,850	2,090*
2. Cash in Register (Start of Month)	100	100	150	70
3. Total Cash (add (1) and (2))	1,500	1,500	2,000	2,160
4. Expected Cash Sales	1,200	1,420	900	
5. Expected Collections	400	380	350	
6. Other Money Expected	100	52	50	
7. Total Receipts (add (4),(5) and (6))	1,700	1,852	1,300	
8. Total Cash and Receipts (add (3) and (7))	3,200	3,352	2,200	
9. All Disbursements (For Month)	1,200	1,192	1,000	
10. Cash Balance at End of Month in Bank Account and Register (Subtract (9) from (8))	2,000	2,160	2,300	

*The owner-manager writes in these figures as they become available.

Cash Flow Schedule - Period of Contract to Repayment of Loan

	July	Aug.	Sept.	Oct.	Nov.
Estimated Receipts					
Cash Sales	800	600	700	1,200	2,800
Accounts Receivable	10,000	10,000	15,800	20,000	31,600
Other Income	200	400	200	480	250
Total Receipts	11,000	11,200	16,700	21,680	34,650
Estimated Disbursements					
Accounts Payable	17,000	11,000	8,200	2,700	2,200
Payroll & Drawing	2,600	4,200	4,200	7,900	5,800
Expenses	1,200	1,800	2,000	2,700	600
Interest Expense	130	130	130	130	130
Plant & Equipment	2,500	460	600	800	100
Reserve for Taxes				3,800*	3,800*
Total Disbursements	23,430	17,590	15,130	18,030	12,630
Estimated Excess Receipts over Disbursements	(12,430)	(6,390)	1,570	3,650	22,020
Estimated Cash Balance at Start of Month	4,200	7,770	1,380	2,950	6,600
Borrowings	16,000				
Loan Repayment					16,000
Estimated Cash Balance at End of Month	7,770	1,380	2,950	6,600	12,620

*To be allotted in October and November so that available cash can be kept at the maximum during the months of heavy cash outflows.

Good managers recognize that occasional borrowing is one of the accepted business tools. Your long range plan for borrowing should be based on the fact that each of the various types of money in your business has its specific and appropriate purpose.

Recognizing this fact is important in preventing the misuse of fund. Keep in mind that misuse can cause a shaky financial operation. This point is especially true when operating cash seeps into long term investment in the business. As a result, the business requires a constant renewal of short term borrowings. Such borrowings indicates a capital deficiency in the business and the need for additional permanent capital.

Bear in mind that financial planning is the first step when borrowing. Such planning must be based on facts that come from your records if you are to secure loans and use them profitably.

F. Special Free Bonuses (with download instructions)

1. Doc Word Format Version of the Business Plan Template

Easily edit and modify it to meet your own specific needs (compatible with most word processors).

Copy the following link to your browser and save the file to your PC:

http://www.bizmove.com/bp/bakery-template.doc

2. An Extensive Generic Business Plan Template In MS Word Format

This is a high quality, full blown business plan template complete with detailed instructions and all related spread sheets. Allows you to prepare a professional business plan for any business.

Copy the following link to your browser and save the file to your PC:

http://www.bizmove.com/tools/Startup-Business-Plan-Template.doc

3. A Set of 23 Excel Spreadsheets and Tables

Use it to create the financial projections, graphs and tables required for a business plan. This includes: start-up expenses, market analysis, sales forecast, personnel plan, financial projections and more.

Copy the following link to your browser and save the file to your PC:

http://www.bizmove.com/bp/spreadseets.xls

4. Business Feasibility Study System

A complete fill in the blanks Business Feasibility Study template system. Featuring crucial things you must consider before you start pouring in your hard earned money, proven to keep you from costly mistakes when starting or expanding a business.

Copy the following link to your browser and save the file to your PC:

http://www.bizmove.com/bp/feasibility.doc

5. Business Financial Planner

This is an easy to use Excel based software program. It is a multi feature financial management program that will help you do the following:

* Plan and analyze your start up expenses and sales

* Perform Break-Even Point analysis

* Conduct 'what-if's analysis

* Perform financial ratios analysis

* Make a "go /no-go" decision

* Create financial projections

Simply type in once your business' details and assumptions and it will automatically produce a comprehensive set of financial projections and analysis for your specific business, including: Start-Up Expenses, Projected Balance Sheet, Projected Cash Flow Statement, Financial Ratios Analysis, Projected Profit and Loss Statement, Break Even Analysis, and many more.

Copy the following link to your browser and save the file to your PC:

http://www.bizmove.com/bp/projections.xlsx

Here's a detailed guide that will walk you step by step and show you exactly how to effectively use the above Business Financial Planner.

Copy the following link to your browser and save the file to your PC:

http://www.bizmove.com/bp/projections-guide.doc

6. How to Improve Your Leadership and Management Skills (eBook)

How to lead and manage people; discover powerful tips and strategies to motivate and inspire your people to bring out the best in them. Be the boss people want to give 200 percent for.

Copy the following link to your browser and save the file to your PC:

http://www.bizmove.com/bp/leadership.pdf

7. Small Business Management: Essential Ingredients for Success (eBook)

Discover scores of business management tricks, secrets and shortcuts. This program does far more than impart knowledge - it inspires action.

Copy the following link to your browser and save the file to your PC:

http://www.bizmove.com/bp/management.pdf

8. How to Create a Business Plan, Training Course (Online Video)

This training course discusses the creation of a business plan. It explains the importance of business planning defines and describes the business plan outline and its components thus enabling you to develop a very good business plan.

Copy the following link to your browser and save the file to your PC:

http://www.bizmove.com/video//business-plan-training-course.htm

9. *How To Find And Attract Investors, Training Course (Online Video):*

This self-paced training video will show you how to find and attract investors. Topics include determining the need for outside financing, defining what an investor is and where to find them, explaining the investment process and understanding investor expectations.

Copy the following link to your browser and save the file to your PC:

http://www.bizmove.com/business-training/how-to-find-and-attract-investors.htm

10. *PowerPoint template to help create a presentation for your business plan.*

Copy the following link to your browser and save the file to your PC:

www.bizmove.com/tools/Business-Plan-Presentation-Template.pptx

* * * *